# The NO-NONSENSE GUIDE to
# ANIMAL RIGHTS

'Publishers have created lists of short books that discuss the questions that your average [electoral] candidate will only ever touch if armed with a slogan and a soundbite. Together [such books] hint at a resurgence of the grand educational tradition... Closest to the hot headline issues are *The No-Nonsense Guides*. These target those topics that a large army of voters care about, but that politicos evade. Arguments, figures and documents combine to prove that good journalism is far too important to be left to (most) journalists.'

Boyd Tonkin,
*The Independent*,
London

**About the author**
**Catharine Grant** is a writer, historian, and activist based in Toronto, Canada. She currently is completing her doctoral dissertation, which compares Ronald Reagan's and Margaret Thatcher's rhetoric on religion, race, gender and sexuality. She is also involved in various campaigns for animal rights, and social and environmental justice.

**Other titles in the series**
*The No-Nonsense Guide to Globalization*
*The No-Nonsense Guide to Climate Change*
*The No-Nonsense Guide to World History*
*The No-Nonsense Guide to Science*
*The No-Nonsense Guide to Conflict and Peace*
*The No-Nonsense Guide to Human Rights*
*The No-Nonsense Guide to Fair Trade*

**About the New Internationalist**
The **New Internationalist** is an independent not-for-profit publishing co-operative. Our mission is to report on issues of global justice. We publish informative current affairs and popular reference titles, complemented by world food, photography and gift books as well as calendars, diaries, maps and posters – all with a global justice world view.

If you like this *No-Nonsense Guide* you'll also love the **New Internationalist** magazine. Each month it takes a different subject such as *Trade Justice*, *Nuclear Power* or *Iraq*, exploring and explaining the issues in a concise way; the magazine is full of photos, charts and graphs as well as music, film and book reviews, country profiles, interviews and news.

To find out more about the **New Internationalist**, visit our website at: **www.newint.org**

The **NO-NONSENSE GUIDE** to

# ANIMAL RIGHTS

**Catharine Grant**

The No-Nonsense Guide to Animal Rights
First published in the UK in 2006 by
New Internationalist™ Publications Ltd
Oxford OX4 1BW, UK
**www.newint.org**
New Internationalist is a registered trade mark.

Cover image: Orangutan. Christer Fredriksson/Lonely Planet Images.

Series editor: Troth Wells
Design by New Internationalist Publications Ltd.

 Printed on recycled paper by T J Press International, Cornwall,
UK who hold environmental accreditation ISO 14001.

British Library Cataloguing-in-Publication Data.
A catalogue record for this book is available from the British Library.

Library of Congress Cataloguing-in-Publication Data.
A catalogue for this book is available from the Library of Congress.

ISBN 10: 1-904456-40-5
ISBN 13: 978-1904456-407

# Foreword

*The individual is capable of both great compassion and great indifference. Humans have it within their means to nourish the former and outgrow the latter... Nothing is more powerful than an individual acting out of conscience, thus helping to bring the collective conscience to life.*

– Norman Cousins (1915-1990),
Journalist and peace activist

I LEFT ENGLAND when I was about 8 years old and went to live in India. There I grew up in a house full of refugees, unwed mothers thrown out of their homes by conservative families, stray dogs, beggar children, ducks discarded from the fairgrounds – you name it. My mother welcomed them all, saying, 'It doesn't matter who is in need, it's that they are in need.' Much later, I came across writer, philosopher and social reformer John Galsworthy's words: 'We are not living in a private world of our own. Everything we say and do and think has its effect on everything around us.'

That's when I realized that this was the most important lesson of my youth, of my life – not my beloved geometry, not that confounding physics, or anything else that I had learned in school. I realized, as writer and naturalist Henry Beston had pointed out many years earlier (in words that I would also cherish) that all of us, no matter our gender, race, religion, nationality, or species, are fellows; whole and complete in our own way, all capable of joy, love, friendship, grief, maternal understanding; the desire to be free and free of pain and fear, and the desire to escape a painful death; and that we are all bundles of emotion.

Animal rights is a marvelous thing, the test of whether we can examine not yesterday's but today's prejudices honestly and reject them as supremacist. It means embracing empathy, that invaluable ability to put oneself in another's place by knocking down those false barriers that place our 'own kind' on one side and 'others' on the other side and replacing them with the golden rule of 'Do unto others' that we humans rightly hold dear in word if not in deed.

Perhaps the hardest thing is not to turn away from the knowledge of what is done to animals in our name, but instead fearlessly to open our hearts and minds to what those 'others' go through, particularly when they go experience it all unwillingly and only because of our unthinking choices in life. The joy is that once we have decided to try to live without causing pain and suffering to animals, it is easy as pie to do. Do not be daunted by the enormity of their plight; rather be glad to have found out what a difference an informed and kind person can make. At PETA, we say, 'Animal liberation is human liberation.' Welcome to your new freedom.

*Ingrid E Newkirk*
Founder of People for the Ethical Treatment of Animals (PETA), and author of *Making Kind Choices*.

# CONTENTS

# Introduction

*The assumption that animals are without rights and the illusion that our treatment of them has no moral significance is a positively outrageous example of Western crudity and barbarity. Universal compassion is the only guarantee of morality.*

– ARTHUR SCHOPENHAUER
(1788-1860), PHILOSOPHER

ANIMALS ARE THE largest group of victims on the planet: more than 50 billion are killed every year to meet human interests. Despite the scientific evidence that shows that all vertebrates are capable of feeling pain and fear, and that many are extremely intelligent, have distinct personalities and are even capable of feeling emotions, many animals are nonetheless denied even the most basic legal protection from harm. Under current laws, inanimate objects and corporations have more legal rights than most animals.[1] It is generally only when animals are considered valuable to humans that the legal system affords them protection.

The animal rights (AR) movement has been one of the fastest growing social movements in history. About 30 years ago, a small group of academics and activists first raised the issue of widespread and systematic animal exploitation, which had largely been ignored by ethicists and animal welfarists alike. Within a decade, thousands of groups around the world, with millions of supporters, became dedicated to promoting animal rights. Today, the AR movement has reached mass dimensions and animal issues are hotly debated in many parts of the world. In 1994, Britain's *Time Out* magazine described animal rights as the number one 'hippest cause'.[2]

The movement considers animals' current status in society to be profoundly unjust. It believes that animals have certain fundamental rights that humans must respect – the right to life, liberty and freedom from unnecessary suffering. Advocates believe that the fact that some animals may be less intelligent than humans is irrelevant to their claim to rights. They argue that to deny animals' rights based on their intellect is morally unjust, and point out that throughout history the oppression of groups often has been based on false assumptions about their intellectual inferiority.

The movement is particularly dismayed by the large-scale abuse of animals in industrial societies. Activists have provided compelling evidence that the entertainment, farming, science and fashion industries have inflicted tremendous suffering. The fact that people are willing to subject so many creatures to pain and confinement suggests to activists that humans need to fundamentally reappraise their relationship with animals.

Because creatures can suffer in many of the same ways that people do, AR activists believe that animals' interests should be considered the moral equivalent of our own. Their ultimate goal is to bring about an end to all animal killing and exploitation. In practical terms, many activists reject the consumption of animal products or by-products, scientific animal testing, using them for entertainment or pleasure, or interfering with them in the wild. These may seem impossible restrictions but AR advocates insist that no matter how humane animal use might be, it is unjust because it disregards animal choice, and physical and psychological wellbeing.

While many advocates feel an intense emotional bond with animals, they insist that this is not a prerequisite for involvement in the movement. They argue that their conviction about animals is primarily the product of a rational ethical position rather than just emotion. AR theorists point out that those who support human rights don't necessarily love

# Introduction

all people but instead believe that all humans have rights regardless of how much or little they contribute to society. Advocates for AR similarly believe that animals have fundamental rights regardless of how cute, loveable or useful they may or may not be to humans. They argue that killing, hurting or confining an animal for any reason violates these fundamental rights and that humans are therefore morally obliged to change the way they perceive animals.

*Catharine Grant*
Toronto, Canada

**1** Lewis Petrinovich, *Darwinian Dominion* (MIT Press, 1999).
**2** People for the Ethical Treatment of Animals, www.peta.org

# 1 Origins of the animal rights movement

*Non-violence leads to the highest ethics, which is the goal of all evolution. Until we stop harming all other living beings, we are still savages.*
   – THOMAS ALVA EDISON (1847-1931), INVENTOR

**As with many other movements, animal rights activism is diverse and broad. Its modern stirrings stem from the broader humanitarian ideals from which it was conceived and it continues to draw upon and influence in equal measure today.**

THE ANIMAL RIGHTS movement identifies with other struggles for justice. Many activists, particularly those involved in the actual liberation of animals, compare themselves with early anti-slavery advocates. Many of the tactics and strategies that the movement uses have been borrowed from earlier historic struggles. Activism has also been profoundly influenced by the animal welfare and environmental movements, which also grant animals moral value.

In a sense, animal rights (AR) evolved out of the concept of animal welfare, which is an old and respected tradition. The first Society for the Prevention of Cruelty to Animals (SPCA) was established in Britain in 1824 to prevent 'wanton' abuse of farm and draft animals. It later campaigned against blood sports, vivisection and inhumane slaughter practices. Mostly organized by people from the upper classes, the welfare movement quickly gained popularity and spread through the Western world. By the end of the 19th century SPCAs and Humane Societies had been established in many American cities as well. Still very active today, the animal welfare movement generally seeks to improve conditions for animals. Welfarists believe that animals are capable of pain, fear and loneliness. However, they also believe that humans and animals exist in a natural hierarchy and that it is appropriate for humans to use animals in responsible ways. They accept the position of animals in society (used for food, clothes, science, companionship and so on) but argue that animals must be treated as humanely as possible. So while animal rightists and welfarists sometimes cooperate on specific issues, because the welfarists generally don't acknowledge that animals have rights, there is tension between the two groups.

### Deep Ecology

'Deep Ecology' has also provided the AR movement with an important foundation. Deep Ecology places high priority on biodiversity, which is the preservation of each and every species on the planet. It recognizes the right of all the elements of nature to exist, regardless of their usefulness to humans. This concept is extremely important for animals because it gives them inherent value independent from human needs and desires. For ecologists, all animals have a key function and are intrinsically valuable.

However, ecologists focus only on the big picture. They don't study individual animals or even single species in isolation but look at broad patterns and relationships. In this sense, Deep Ecology embraces a fundamentally different philosophy from the AR movement. While AR advocates take seriously the suffering of every individual animal, ecologists are mostly interested in the health of entire ecosystems. They aren't necessarily concerned about the suffering of individual animals if the population as a whole is healthy.[1]

Wildlife conservationists also give priority to vulnerable wild populations. Because domesticated animals are abundant and tend to interfere with natural ecosystems, they are not considered worthy of protection. In addition, conservationists consider non-sentient life (organisms that aren't self-aware – plants, for example) to be equally important to the health of ecosystems and don't necessarily give priority to sentient animals over non-sentient life. For the AR movement an animal's ability to feel pain or unhappiness is an essential reason why it should have certain rights.[2]

So while the movement has drawn strength from the animal welfare and Deep Ecology groupings, it differs in significant ways. It puts value on all animals, not just those that comprise 'nature', and grants them rights as opposed to just protection.

## Birth of the movement

Australian-born ethicist Peter Singer is considered by many to be the founder of the animal rights movement. His groundbreaking book, *Animal Liberation*, was first published in 1975. Within a year, the British-based Animal Liberation Front (ALF) had been established, and by the end of the decade several other animal liberation organizations had been created. Hundreds of thousands of copies of the book have been sold and it has been translated into nine languages.[3]

While animal liberation is not synonymous with animal rights (as will be discussed below), most well-known activists acknowledge that Singer's work had a profound effect on them.

Singer criticizes 'speciesism' (a term coined by his colleague Richard Ryder) – the human readiness to treat a creature of another species in a way that one wouldn't be willing to treat a member of our own species. Singer believes that attempts to improve conditions for animals are admirable but argues that they are 'based on quite conventional ways of thinking about the status of animals'.[4]

Essentially, Singer challenges this conventional

thinking by suggesting that because animals are just as capable of suffering as humans, their interests should be given the same consideration as our own. While the welfare movement encourages people to be kind to animals, it doesn't require humans to give up their domination. It seeks to increase our obligation toward animals, whereas the AR movement insists that animals have moral status.

Singer was not the first to reappraise how we relate to animals, he was simply the first to inspire an international movement. Nearly a century earlier, the British humanitarian Henry Salt called for the equal consideration of humans and animals. Indeed, Singer was inspired by Salt's work and reprinted his 1892 work *Animal Rights, Considered in Relation to Social Progress*. Salt was a radical thinker for his time and he dedicated his life to reducing the suffering of humans and non-humans. For Salt, as with many other early animal activists, the plight of oppressed humans was intimately connected with that of animals. He argued that human suffering could not truly be eradicated while animal suffering continued. Through his Humanitarian League, Salt advocated vegetarianism and campaigned for the abolition of vivisection, hunting and the abuse of animals 'for fashion, in farms, markets and slaughterhouses'.[5]

Because he rejected the use of animals for human purposes, Salt was much more radical than his peers in the SPCA.

There were other important developments in the 20th century that contributed to the AR movement. A century earlier, some social reformers had rejected the consumption of meat because they believed it contributed to malnutrition among the working class (because meat requires more resources to produce than plant-based foods). By the mid-20th century, vegetarian societies, which rejected meat-eating for *ethical* reasons, were well-established. Influential vegetarians like George Bernard Shaw and Mahatma Gandhi advocated a 'humane diet' in their circles and to the public at large. The principle of 'veganism' – a diet that avoids all animal products, including milk and eggs – was established during the Second World War. While veganism remained uncommon for most of the 20th century, vegetarianism grew after World War Two, was particularly embraced by the counter-culture in the 1960s, and finally reached mass proportions in the 1980s.

But Singer's book was important because it inspired a cohesive, international movement committed to ending animal exploitation. Scholars such as Ruth Harrison, Stanley and Roslind Godlovitch, John Harris, and Richard Ryder, who had already written about various forms of animal oppression, became much more involved after the publication of *Animal Liberation*, and people became increasingly aware of the industrialized abuse of animals. Singer's work also encouraged the publication of hundreds more studies of the treatment of animals in society, the philosophical and legal debates surrounding animal rights, and the development of animal welfare as a scientific field.

## Approaches to animal rights

The AR movement has various approaches and philosophical bases. Despite his importance to the movement, Singer does not advocate the classic rights position. Rather, he argues that animals should be given equal consideration with humans. Tom Regan, on the other hand, is the architect of the actual animal rights position, which has been adopted by so many activists. Regan argues that animals should hold the same fundamental moral rights as humans.[6]

While Singer believes that the degree of animal suffering in society cannot be justified in terms of how much it benefits humans, Regan believes that any kind of animal use, even if it is relatively benign, violates animals' fundamental rights. However, while Singer and Regan's positions differ philosophically, both consider the exploitation of animals in society to be unjust and have worked to end it.

Another important approach is articulated by Steven Wise, a lawyer who is working to get Great Apes considered as persons under the law. Wise argues that the Great Apes are so similar to humans that it is unjust to deny them legal rights based on their species. Not only do apes share 99 per cent of our DNA, but they are intellectually comparable. Chimpanzees, for example, are cognitively superior to infant humans: they can count, learn human language, make and use tools, and recognize themselves in mirrors.

Like humans, apes are also capable of acts of altruism. They will defend each other, help tend wounds and look after orphaned babies. Other animals, such as elephants and *cetaceans* (whales, dolphins and porpoises) also share these characteristics. Wise believes that such creatures deserve the same legal protection as humans. He hopes that if the species barrier between humans and our closest living relatives can be transcended, then eventually other animals, even those with fewer 'human' qualities, will also be granted rights under the law. Wise teaches animal rights law at Harvard University, and attempts to provide legal representation for animals whose rights he believes have been violated. He hopes that within the next 20 years, apes will be recognized as legal subjects.[7]

Peter Singer and others have also done this kind of work through the Great Apes Project.

There are thousands of groups around the world working on a variety of issues using very different tactics. Some of the largest and most successful organizations are able to run multiple campaigns, and focus on many aspects of the human/animal relationship.

People for the Ethical Treatment of Animals (PETA) is probably the most influential international such organization. Established in 1980 by Ingrid Newkirk and Alex Pacheco, it now has almost one million members worldwide. With a staff of over 100 and an annual budget exceeding $25 million, PETA has chapters in the US, the Netherlands, Germany, Britain and India among other countries. It has outreach and education programs, and also conducts investigations and legal proceedings against companies that have low welfare standards.

However, the organization is best known for its controversial advertising campaigns and shock tactics. PETA frequently uses celebrities, nude models and extremely disturbing images to generate interest in animal rights. One of its main strategies has been to publicly shame companies into altering the way they treat animals. It has managed to pressure many corporate giants, like General Motors, Revlon and McDonald's, into changing their practices. While the organization regularly generates controversy, it is nonetheless extremely professional. Not only does PETA provide thousands of free resources to anyone interested in the issues, but it also provides reams of scientific and professional evidence to support its claims.

### Animal liberation

The Animal Liberation Front (ALF) is the most controversial animal rights group, even within the movement itself. Established in Britain in 1976 by Ronnie Lee, it now has branches in the US, Australia, New Zealand/Aotearoa, France, Italy, Spain, Poland, Sweden, South Africa and Canada.[8]

ALF members engage in illegal direct action in order to rescue animals and damage facilities that are involved in animal exploitation (such as research facilities, breeding facilities, slaughterhouses and fur farms). While the ALF rejects the use of violence, it does condone property damage and theft. Its activists argue that they are following a higher moral law when they break property and trespass laws to liberate animals.

'Over the years, its actions have set free thousands of animals, caused billions of dollars in damage, and exposed some of the worst animal abuses to the public,' reported *The Guardian* newspaper. The organization's activities are funded entirely by individual donors, and to avoid infiltration by the police it has no central organization or coordination. Its activists have been jailed and the FBI considers the organization 'our highest domestic terrorism investigation priority.'[9]

In both Britain and the US, terrorism laws recently have been amended to target direct action groups like the ALF. These laws make it easier for the State to prosecute and imprison individuals who damage the property to industries that exploit animals. In Australia, however, there is much less stigma attached to the notion of animal liberation.[10] One Australian organization, called Animal Liberation, has eight chapters nationwide. While the organization is not affiliated to the ALF, it nonetheless espouses a radical rights position.

In addition to the hundreds of multi-issue animal

---

### Do animal activists care about humans?

The majority of early reformers who worked to end animal suffering were also active in other forms of philanthropy. Many 19th century suffragettes and abolitionists were active in the anti-vivisection campaign, and some social reformers were involved in promoting animal welfare. This trend has continued into the contemporary period. Studies of donation patterns show that people concerned with animal issues are also concerned with human issues and are likely to donate their money to organizations that help people as well as those that help animals. ■

Richard Ryder, *The Political Animal* (McFarland, 1998).

rights groups around the world, there are thousands of organizations dedicated to working on single issues, such as animal experimentation, hunting and factory farming. These groups choose to direct their energy to things that affect a large number of animals. As they focus on specific issues, many such groups have had a significant impact on public attitudes.

The emergence of the AR movement has had a radicalizing effect on some of the mainstream animal welfare organizations. The Humane Society of the United States (HSUS) and the British Royal Society for the Prevention of Cruelty to Animals (RSPCA), two large and very influential organizations, have changed their positions in the last two decades because of pressure from the movement. While they used to have fairly conservative animal protection policies and tried to avoid challenging industrial uses of animals, they have now come out in support of much more far-reaching measures in all areas of society and the economy. In some respects, their policies are nearly identical to those of the major AR organizations.

This is illustrated by the fact that Robin Webb, a spokesperson for the ALF, was on the board of directors of the RSPCA in the 1990s, while Liz White, an animal rights activist, headed the Toronto Humane Society, the largest in Canada. The radicalization of the animal movement has been a significant development because the large welfare organizations are respected by policy-makers and the public. Welfare groups are considered more respectable and less threatening than AR groups, and are therefore much more likely to influence government policy.

Almost every country has at least one organization that tries to protect animals in one way or another. In many places, particularly in the US, Australia, India, and Western Europe, animal activists are becoming increasingly aware of the ethical limitations of traditional animal welfare and have embraced the rights position. The public is becoming increasingly interested in these issues. Just as politically conscious people have become educated about the exploitative labor practices and environmental degradation inherent in the global economic system, they are also starting to question industrial animal exploitation, which has steadily increased in the last 50 years.

**1** Lewis Petrinovich, *Darwinian Dominion* (MIT Press, 1999). **2** Eugene Hargrove (ed.), *The Animal Rights/Environmental Ethics Debate* (State University of New York, 1992). **3** Charlotte Montgomery, *Blood Relations* (Between the Lines, 2000). **4** Peter Singer, *Animal Liberation*, 3rd edition (Pimlico, 1995). **5** Mark Gold, *Animal Century* (Jon Carpenter, 1998). **6** Tom Regan has written extensively on the subject of animal rights. See *All That Dwell Therein* (University of California Press, 1982), *The Case for Animal Rights* (Temple University Press, 1983), *The Struggle for Animal Rights* (International Society for Animal Rights, 1987), *Defending Animal Rights* (University of Illinois Press, 2001), *Empty Cages* (Rowman and Littlefield, 2004). **7** Steven Wise, 'A Legal Person', in *Animal Rights: Current Debates and New Directions* ed Cass R Sunstein, Martha C Nussbaum (Nature/OUP, 2004). **8** Robert Garner, *Animals, politics and morality* (Manchester University Press, 1993). **9** *The Guardian*, 21 July 2004. **10** Richard Ryder, *The Political Animal* (McFarland, 1998).

# 2 A Western, middle-class phenomenon?

*The greatness of a nation and its moral progress can be judged by the way its animals are treated.*
— MOHANDAS K (MAHATMA) GANDHI (1869-1948), INDIAN INDEPENDENCE LEADER

**Caring for animals is not just a whim of the privileged few nor is it particularly 'Western' or middle-class. People all over the world, from many different backgrounds and cultures, consider it important to protect animals.**

SOME CRITICS OF the AR movement suggest that it is an exclusively Western phenomenon, which places more importance on animals than on the cultures and needs of people around the world. They argue that promoting animal interests is a form of cultural imperialism, which imposes Western values on non-Western peoples.[1]

In one sense, these critics are correct: the movement is strongest in the West. However, some argue that this has less to do with culture than with material wellbeing. Western democracies tend to have well-developed social programs, rarely suffer from famine or war and enjoy high levels of education and standards of living. While some studies show that poor people are among the most charitable, sociologist David Nibert argues that those living in acute insecurity are forced to focus mostly on their own survival, as opposed to the wellbeing of any other oppressed group.[2] On the other hand, studies have shown that people who are physically and economically secure are more likely to show empathy toward others, including animals. Attitudes towards animals seem to be more connected to prosperity than they are to culture and tend to change once a society becomes more stable and affluent.

While some activists have been critical of cultures that engage in subsistence animal use (see chapter 7), the movement has been even more critical of Western attitudes towards animals. Some academics and activists have argued that animal rights are, in many ways, contrary to Western traditions. They suggest that the underlying principles of the movement have in fact been inherited from Eastern traditions, and that many people outside the rich world practice day-to-day animal rights as a matter of course. While the British writer Henry Salt may have coined the term 'animal rights', he certainly didn't come up with the concept.

## Religion
Many activists have lamented the fact that Judeo-Christianity, the central religious culture in the West, seems to justify the subjugation of animals. While some people have interpreted the Bible as advocating kindness and compassion towards animals (think of St Francis of Assisi), the dominant theological interpretation is that in the Bible (Genesis) God authorized humans to have 'dominion' over them. According to this interpretation, which was codified by St Thomas Aquinas, because humans were formed in God's image they have higher spiritual value than animals. Aquinas (and Augustine and Aristotle before him) believed that animals had no souls and that it therefore was impossible to sin against them.[3]

Because Aquinas had so much influence over the development of Christianity, through history the mistreatment of animals has been 'sanctioned as the will of God'.[2] While Christianity and Judaism emphasize kindness towards other humans, animals fall outside the realm of moral consideration.[4] According to Anglican priest Andrew Linzey, the dominant Judeo-Christian tradition has discouraged reflection on the position of animals in society.[5]

Some major religions of the East, such as Jainism, Hinduism and Buddhism, have a very different approach to animals. These religions emphasize *ahimsa*, which is the principle of non-violence towards all living things. The first precept is a prohibition against the killing of any creature. The Jain, Hindu and Buddhist injunctions against killing serve to teach that all creatures are spiritually equal. An act of violence against an animal is considered the moral equivalent to an act of violence against a human. While religious strictures only go so far in preventing violence, it is still an important societal influence that both human and animal rights campaigners in the East make use of in their advocacy work.

The three religions also believe that living creatures are fundamentally interconnected. All creatures exist in a cycle of death and rebirth and can be reincarnated in various forms. Animals can be reborn as humans and humans can be reborn as animals because there is no distinct spiritual difference between the two. For this reason, Jains, Hindus and Buddhists emphasize compassion to all animals.

## A Western, middle-class phenomenon?

There are about 4 million Jains in India today. As a religious principle, they do everything that they can to minimize animal suffering. They are strict vegetarians who eat as low down on the food chain as possible.[5] Almost every Jain community in India has established animal hospitals where injured or abandoned animals are cared for, and they periodically rescue animals from slaughterhouses. Jains even do their best to avoid stepping on or ingesting insects by mistake. They believe that minimizing suffering is a spiritual necessity.

Buddha's disapproval of killing has been interpreted differently by various Buddhist schools. However, the most prominent Buddhist sect, Mahayana, which is widely practiced in China, Hong Kong, Vietnam, Korea and Taiwan, explicitly prohibits the killing of animals. Contemporary Mahayana Buddhists are vegetarian; monks and nuns also avoid leather (and sometimes dairy) products. Mahayana emphasizes Buddha's teaching on compassion to animals and maintains that we can only escape our own suffering if we avoid inflicting it on others.[6] Mahayana is the largest Buddhist school, with over 200 million members worldwide. However, unlike Jains, Mahayana Buddhists do not prohibit the keeping of pets. Caged wild animals are commonly held at Buddhist temples in Asia.

### Hinduism

Hinduism was distinctly influenced by Jainism and Buddhism, both of which originated in India. As teachings on compassion became widespread within the Hindu tradition, followers adopted ethical vegetarianism. Hindu scripture emphasizes that 'the meat of other animals is like eating the flesh of one's son'[7] and that all animals are a part of God.[5] The majority of Indians are now vegetarian because of their spiritual beliefs. Of the 800,000,000 Hindus in India, more than 80 per cent are vegetarian. Hindus venerate a variety of animals, such as tigers and elephants, but also more common animals, like mice and snakes.[8] The cow is particularly sacred; Hindus respect it because it is essential to small-scale subsistence agriculture, still widespread in India. Not only do cows provide milk and labor but their manure is an important source of fertilizer and fuel. Hindus are grateful to the cow for providing for their needs and in return treat it with honor.[4]

India is one of the few countries that has animal welfare provisions written into its constitution. Mahatma Gandhi, the founding father of independent India, advocated compassion to all living things. He publicly opposed eating meat, animal experimentation and all forms of cruelty to animals.

Gandhi's influence has been profound. While animal exploitation certainly does occur in India, the country has a particularly strong animal rights movement. There are hundreds of animal protection and AR organizations there. Two of the most influential are Blue Cross and People for Animals (which has an astounding 72 groups in India). British-based Beauty Without Cruelty and American-based PETA also have vibrant Indian chapters that tackle local issues. Many Indian AR organizations draw on the country's cultural and religious heritage to get their message across, and have the support of celebrities, the media and the Government. There are primetime TV programs dedicated to animal welfare issues. Hosted by Maneka Gandhi, the founder of People for Animals, *Head or Tails* and *Maneka's Ark* have a weekly audience of 200 million. Gandhi also has a weekly radio program and her columns on animals appear in 20 newspapers.[9]

## Changing attitudes in Asia

While Southeast Asia has a bad reputation in the West for its treatment of animals, the movement is growing there as well. A 2005 Mori Poll found that 90 per cent of people in the region believe that humans have a moral duty to minimize animal suffering and that laws

## A Western, middle-class phenomenon?

should reflect this. The BBC reported that 'millions of people in Asia think animal welfare is important'.[10]

Despite a dearth of animal welfare laws, China has well-established traditions of compassion to animals. Not only do Mahayana Buddhists practice it as a religious duty, but historically, rural Chinese have respected and valued animals. However, while the standard of living rose in the West over the last century, in China – as in much of the developing world – people faced poverty and political repression. Chronic insecurity has made it difficult for many Chinese to focus on anything other than their own wellbeing. However, in the last ten years, animal welfare organizations have made significant progress there. Organizations like the International Fund for Animal Welfare, World Wide Fund for Nature (WWF), World Society for the Protection of Animals, and Compassion in World Farming (CIWF) are now flourishing in China.

### Asiatic bear farming

The Chinese Government has also started to listen to public opinion on animal issues. In May 2004, it was forced to cancel plans to bring bullfighting to Beijing as a result of public outcry.[11] Another pivotal issue has been the Asiatic bear bile industry. Bears' bile has medicinal properties and has been used in traditional medicine for thousands of years. Bear farming was introduced in the 1980s to take pressure off the endangered wild population. However, because bear-farming causes suffering and synthetic and herbal substitutes do exist, the Chinese authorities – under pressure from animal groups – agreed in 1994 to stop granting bear-farm licenses. In addition, in 2000 the Government agreed to release 500 of China's 7,000 farmed bears to sanctuaries operated by Animals Asia. Saving the 'China bear' has now become a matter of national pride for the Chinese public. The media and local celebrities are supporting the campaign and medical schools in Beijing and Szechuan have agreed to stop using bear bile in medical treatments.[12]

Caring for animals is not just a Western whim.[10] People all over the globe, from a variety of cultures and traditions, consider it important to protect animals from human exploitation. The fact that there are animal protection organizations in almost every country in the world reflects this. From anti-vivisection groups in Japan, to elephant sanctuaries in Thailand, to stray cat and dog rescues in Brazil, to wildlife preservation in Tanzania, people everywhere believe that animals are worth protecting. And while Western thinkers have considered the plight of animals over the last couple of centuries, some Eastern traditions have encouraged compassion and even basic rights for animals for thousands of years.

1 George Wenzel, *Animal Rights, Human Wrongs* (University of Toronto Press, 1991). 2 David Nibert, *Animal Rights, Human Rights* (Rowman and Littlefield, 2002). 3 Colin Spencer, *The Heretic's Feast*, (University Press of New England, 1995). 4 Stephen Rosen, *Diet for Transcendence*, (Torchlight, 1997). 5 Rynn Berry, *Food for the Gods*, (Pythagorean, 1998). 6 Interview with Venerable Yung Ku, Abbess at Fo Guan Shan Temple (Toronto, 2005). 7 Quoted in *Nonviolence to Animals, Earth and Self in Asian Traditions*, Christopher Chapple (State University of New York, 1993). 8 'Tigerland', Bittu Sagha, *New Internationalist* No 288, March 1997. 9 Mark Gold, *Animal Century*, (Jon Carpenter, 1998). 10 BBC News, 'Asia "wakes up" to animal welfare', http://news.bbc.co.uk 11 'A Roar from Animal Activists in China', Mark Magnier, *The Boston Globe*, www.boston.com/news/ 12 Jill Robinson, Director of Animals Asia, lecture at Earthrangers, 2004.

# 3 Food animals

*A diet higher in whole grains and legumes and lower in beef and other meat is not just healthier for ourselves but also contributes to changing the world system that feeds some people and leaves others hungry.*
— DR WALDEN BELLO (1945-   ), ACTIVIST

**From the farm to the fork, the increasingly globalized production and consumption of animal-based food is wreaking havoc on the world's ecosystems, gobbling up scarce resources and damaging people's health.**

THE MAJORITY OF animals killed by humans today are those raised for food. Not including fish, 25 billion food animals are slaughtered every year worldwide. Many activists argue that, in this day and age, it is fundamentally wrong to raise animals to eat their flesh, or the other foodstuffs that they produce, such as milk or eggs. They argue that humans can survive and flourish without eating animal products. They also point out that farming has become increasingly cruel and exploitative in the past 50 years. Even animal welfarists who don't inherently oppose the human consumption of meat, point out that conditions for the majority of livestock have become intolerable because of the increasing industrialization and globalization of farming.

Through history, up to the mid-20th century, most people in the West had some interaction with farm animals. Until the post-World War Two period, most animals in Europe and North America were raised on small, family-run farms and slaughtering and processing facilities were locally-based industries. Today, the meat, egg and dairy industries advertise their products with bucolic images of small farms, where sheep and cattle live in pastures or in straw-filled barns. Conditions have likely never been quite as idyllic as these images suggest, but certainly bear little resemblance to the modern factory farms where most livestock are now reared. These creatures live and die away from public scrutiny: many Westerners are now far removed from the animals they eat and may have little idea how and where these are raised and slaughtered.

A typical farm no longer has barns and pastures, but rather windowless sheds where animals are treated like industrial machines. Today, slaughterhouses are high-security facilities surrounded by walls and barbed wire, and use assembly-line techniques to kill and dismember animals. And as Western-style factory farming supplants traditional agriculture in the South, this trend is also increasingly common there also.

## Conditions for farmed animals

The nature of farming has changed dramatically since the end of the Second World War. In North America for example, in the 1950s, new technology, prosperity and increased consumption led to a major consolidation of farming, a pattern followed in other parts of the rich world. Agriculture, which had been diverse and local, became increasingly monocultural (ie focusing on one crop or type of animal) and centralized. Part of the impetus for this was the growth of the fast food industry. McDonald's is the biggest buyer of beef in the US.

In the 1970s, the company decided that it needed a uniform product and stopped buying from multiple suppliers. As a result, only the biggest livestock producers were able to stay in business.[1] The process of agricultural consolidation reached its peak in the mid-1980s. Today, a handful of corporations control the majority of livestock farms in North America and around the world.

As a result, most of the animals and animal products we eat come from huge industrial farms that operate like factories. The purpose of 'factory farming' is to produce the most meat, dairy or eggs as quickly and as cheaply as possible. The more a company produces, the more it can lower its prices. This, in turn, encourages the public to consume more which results in more business, and more profits, for the producer. Here's how a US pork-industry journal, *Hog Farm Management*, puts it: 'Forget the pig is an animal. Treat it just like a machine in a factory. Schedule treatments like you would lubrication. Breeding season is the first step in an assembly line. And marketing like the delivery of finished goods.'[2]

There are two major strategies for producing cheap animal products. First, producers house their livestock in the smallest possible space because this substantially reduces labor costs. If animals are kept inside cages in a warehouse that has mechanized feeding and lighting, it takes very few workers to care for them. In a factory farm, one worker can care for thousands of animals, and tens of thousands of birds.[3]

Because producers try to pack in as many animals as possible, the conditions are abysmal for the majority of 'intensively produced' livestock. Most pigs, for example, are raised on 'farms' that contain more than 5,000 animals.[4] To make this possible, they are kept in stalls so small that they can't move or turn around, and because they are so crowded, their ears and tails are docked (without anesthetic) so that they won't get chewed on. They live on concrete or wire floors instead of on dirt or straw (because it is easier to clean), and often develop painful deformities in their legs and hooves.

The average broiler chicken warehouse holds 45,000 hens.[5] The chickens are packed in wire cages so small that they don't have room to move or stretch their wings. They are de-beaked (without anesthetic) so that they don't peck each other to death in their cramped conditions. About half the dairy cows in the

US are kept permanently indoors, and have never gone out to pasture. Steers raised for beef are de-horned (without anesthetic) so that they don't gore each other in over-crowded feedlots and transport trucks.

## Drugs and disease

In order to survive factory farm conditions, animals must be kept permanently medicated with antibiotics. Housing is so cramped and often dirty that disease is rampant. Half of the antibiotics produced in the world every year are used on farms to keep livestock alive.[6] However millions do not survive. In the UK about 2.7 million turkeys die in their sheds before slaughter every year.[5] In 2001, 22 of Canada's 780 federally inspected slaughterhouses reported that they received 7,382 cattle and 4,684 pigs that had become mortally sick or injured on the farms they came from.[7] It is common for egg farms to lose 10-15 per cent of its hens every year due to poor conditions and stress[8] and 70 per cent of pigs arrive at slaughterhouses with pneumonia, caused by the high level of ammonia in their poorly ventilated indoor stalls.[3]

Factory farmed animals are also altered so that they will produce more of the meat that is particularly appealing to consumers. Chickens, for example, have been bred to grow abnormally large breasts, because breasts have the highest retail value. However, their skeletons do not grow with their body mass, which means that their frames cannot support their weight. Such chickens are highly susceptible to broken limbs. Despite the fact that they are herbivores, beef cattle are 'finished' with high protein diets, which commonly include animal byproducts and manure. They are also fed growth hormones so that they will gain the maximum amount of weight and sell for a higher price. Pigs are prevented from moving so that their flesh remains tender and they won't burn calories and lose weight. Veal calves are fed iron-deficient feed

## Food animals

(that gives them chronic diarrhea) so that their meat will remain pale and expensive. Ducks and geese are mechanically force-fed so that their livers will be fatty and bloated enough to produce *fois gras*. Dairy cows are treated with hormones so that they will carry up to ten times more milk than they would naturally.[5]

Around the world, the majority of animals raised for food are farmed highly intensively. Traditional farming has become the exception to the rule. Danielle Nierenberg of the Worldwatch Institute estimates that more than half of the world's pork and poultry, and 43 per cent of the world's beef, is raised on factory farms.[9] In the US, 90 per cent of all meat is produced in this way.[10] While such farming has long dominated

---

### 'Mad cow' and foot and mouth

The 'Mad cow' (BSE) and foot and mouth (FMD) epidemics in the UK were both the result of intensive farming. 'Mad cow' disease – *bovine spongiform encephalopathy* (BSE) – involves the progressive degeneration of the central nervous system. While the origins of the disease are unclear, scientists know that it is spread by feeding livestock parts of other infected animals (particularly the brain, spinal cord and retina). In other words, BSE would never have reached epidemic proportions if livestock producers had not insisted on feeding the cheapest available protein (basically swept up from the slaughterhouse floor) to their herbivores. Since the disease was discovered in 1986, 4.7 million adult cattle and 1.98 million immature beasts have been destroyed in Britain, in the hope of eradicating the illness, which can be contracted by people who eat the tainted meat.[1] However because the incubation period for BSE is anywhere between 2-12 years, and the practice of feeding livestock to other livestock is so widespread, the disease is still rampant. There are recorded cases throughout Europe (and still in the UK) and North America. Millions of animals have died because they were forced to eat meat, when they are naturally vegetarian.

FMD existed before the advent of factory farming. However, these days it flourishes in intensive conditions because it can be transmitted through the air, and factory farm warehouses are overcrowded and generally poorly ventilated. In 1998 the UN warned that Europe was likely to have an outbreak of the disease because of large-scale animal movement and overcrowding. It declared that 'the globalization and intensification of agriculture has led to an increased risk and

production in North America, Europe and Japan, it has recently begun to take root in other parts of the world – particularly in the former Soviet Union, Mexico, Brazil, India, China, Thailand and the Philippines. Just as the industry has moved South to maximize profits at the expense of local peoples and ecosystems, agri-businesses are also opening factory farms in countries where labor and environmental standards are less rigid. US-owned Smithfield Foods, the largest pork producer in the world, has recently opened plants in Mexico and Poland. While the Mexican Government has been cooperative, the Polish authorities tried to stop Smithfield's expansion because local farmers worried that competition from

increasing frequency of livestock disease epidemics'. Britain suffered an epidemic in 2001, during which over 2 million farm animals with the disease were culled. As a result of the ban on movement, a further 1.5 million were killed because they couldn't be moved to adequate housing.[2,3]

However, the cull was not necessary: FMD does not pose a health risk to humans, and animals cease to be contagious after 8 days. But the long-term effects of the illness include weight reduction and lower milk production and conception rates. The US Department of Agriculture (USDA) reports that 'animals do not normally regain lost weight for many months. Recovered cows seldom produce milk at their former rates.'[4] Cattle are considered economic units, as opposed to living creatures, and so the decision to cull them made economic sense. Producers stood to lose money from less 'productive' animals and the cheapest solution was a massive cull. As *The New York Times* reported, FMD was an 'economic disease'.[5]

Animals that aren't raised intensively are also at risk from livestock epidemics. During the recent avian flu outbreak, over 100 million fowl were culled in an attempt to contain the virus. While the outbreak originated on overcrowded, dirty and poorly ventilated, indoor chicken farms, even organic and free-range farmers were forced to destroy their livestock. In this sense, factory farming puts all farm animals at risk.[6] ∎

Sources: 1 Animal Aid, 'Close Up On BSE', www.animalaid.org 2 *The Guardian*, 19 June 2004. 3 Friends of the Earth, www.foe.co.uk 4 USDA Veterinary Services, Factsheet, January 2002. 5 *The New York Times*, 6 May 2001. 6 United Poultry Concerns, 'Avian Influenza Update', www.upc-online.org

# The real cost of a factory-farmed egg

A female chick hatched in a large-scale egg-laying factory will be de-beaked without anesthetic within the first few days of her life. This is so she will not peck the other birds with whom she shares her shoebox-sized cage. Her de-beaking may cause a painful condition called neuroma, whereby a mass of intertwining nerves grows back after the beak has been cut. Producers believe that the practice is 'efficient' – it only costs $0.10 to take off a chick's beak. Paying for the space and labor to keep hens in less crowded conditions would cost the producer more.

An egg-laying hen will likely be fed the remains of all the male chicks that hatch at the plant because these provide cheap and easy protein and are byproducts of the industry. Only the female chicks are kept alive because they produce eggs. Because it is her instinct to dust-bathe, a hen often ends up with sores and lacerations on her breasts, as she tries to simulate dust bathing by rubbing against the cage. She may also develop leg and foot deformities when her claws grow around the wire bottom of her cage, which is designed this way so her excrement will fall easily through the bottom. If she is particularly unlucky, she'll get her head caught in the wire and will eventually starve to death for being unable to reach food. Because there are so many chickens in these 'battery' operations, individual monitoring or even corpse removal is impractical. As a result, the average industrialized 'hen house' is full of dying chickens and corpses. One observer commented that 'corpses are everywhere'.[1]

To ensure that hens lay eggs continually, producers use a regimen called 'forced molting'. Hens are deprived of food for 6-10 days and then have it gradually reintroduced. After molting, reproductive rates peak and another egg-laying cycle begins. About 10 per cent of hens die during this process.

After a year or so, a hen is worn out. Her natural life span is up to 10 years but due to intensive laying – she will have produced more than 300 – her eggs have become watery and no longer meet industry standards. Egg-laying hens do not see natural daylight until this point, when they are transported to the slaughterhouse. They can be legally transported without food and water for up to 72 hours. Because continual egg-laying causes a weakening of the bones, a hen may well break a limb during transport. About 15 per cent of hens die from illness, injury and stress, on their way to slaughter. On the 'kill floor', the hens are hung upside-down on an assembly line, and depending on where they have been raised, they may be slaughtered after being stunned with an electrical current or while fully conscious. ∎

Source: 1 Nathan Noblis, 'The Abuse of Science by Canadian and US Egg Industries', Two Days of Thinking About Animals (conference), Brock University, 2005.

the huge corporation would force them to give up their traditional farming methods. The head of the Polish Farmers' Union, who supported the Government's decision, said: 'These are concentration camps for hogs... We had concentration camps in Poland before. We will not allow them again...' Local activists were unwilling to give up their autonomy as independent farmers. However the giant corporation out-maneuvered the Government by using local front companies to buy over 30 sites to produce pork.[11]

## Animals, Inc.

Livestock production is dominated by a few large corporations. For example, in the US, four companies control 79 per cent of the beef industry; two of those companies, Cargill and IBP, also own 74 per cent of Canada's beef industry.[12] Cargill also controls much of the Australian beef industry, while the giant ConAgra controls most large-scale poultry production in China and Thailand.[2] Some individual farmers are indeed committed to ensuring a reasonable standard of care for their animals. However, they are being pushed out of business by their corporate competitors, because they are unable to produce livestock as cheaply. Corporate farming has replaced family farming in most of the world.

The largest meatpacker companies are 'vertically integrated', which means they own both production and processing (and sometimes even distribution and retail) facilities. This provides corporations with the opportunity to squeeze extra profits out of animals in the transportation and slaughtering process. Those that survive the ordeal of the 'farm' have then to make the journey to the slaughterhouse. This can take days, as animals are often reared in concentrated pockets and then distributed throughout countries and even continents. Some countries export the majority of their live animals to others. Australia is the largest live

## Food animals

animal exporter – every year it sends over 7 million animals overseas, particularly to the Middle East.[10] As well as truck or rail transport, these animals also have to survive days at sea. There have been several disasters over the years, such as ships sinking and journeys taking so long that the majority of the animals perish. The global trade in livestock has greatly increased their suffering.

Animals can be kept in transport vehicles without food, water or rest for anywhere between 28 and 72 hours. Because of stress and overcrowding, lack of nourishment and temperature control, many animals get sick, are injured, and even die. In Canada alone, every year 3.5 million animals arrive at slaughterhouses dead or dying from transport conditions. Most frequently they suffer from heart attacks, broken limbs, dehydration, and freezing.[13]

## Down and out
However in many countries it is now illegal for slaughterhouses to process dead or dying animals. Known as 'downers', most are either 'spent' dairy cattle who suffer from broken limbs because they are particularly susceptible to osteoporosis, or pigs who have died of heart attacks from the stress of transport. In order to be legally slaughtered, an animal must be able to walk through the slaughterhouse doors, so staff are encouraged to get sick and injured animals back on their feet. Workers often kick, drag and electrically shock 'downed' animals to get them moving. If an animal is too ill or injured to move it is dragged out of the truck by bulldozer and left to die – there is no mercy killing at a slaughterhouse.[14]

Once inside, things get even worse. Profit motives have relentlessly increased processing speeds, resulting in incredible suffering for livestock. The largest slaughterhouses now butcher some 2,000 animals every hour. In most countries, it is required by law to stun livestock before slaughter (poultry are excluded from this in the US and Australia, and some countries have exemptions for religious slaughtering rituals). However, because of the frenetic pace, many animals aren't stunned properly before they are butchered. Reports from major media outlets recount horror stories of animals being hoisted by the leg onto the conveyor belt and skinned alive. Even the best slaughterhouses have been found to usually miss about 5 per cent of the animals that go through the 'stun room'.[2] That means that millions of cows, pigs and sheep are disassembled while conscious in North America every year. They die in agony and surrounded by blood, offal, and the screams of other animals.

As with livestock, fishing has become heavily industrialized. It has also become dominated by large corporations such as Mitsubishi and Heinz.[15] Nearly 100 million tons of seafood is caught every year. Of the 12 million fishers in the world today, 11 million use traditional technologies to catch half of this. The other half is caught by the one million who work on 37,000 commercial ocean trawlers.[15] Corporate overfishing has resulted in serious depletion of all the world's major fishing areas. More than 1,000 species

## Fishing and 'bushmeat' in Africa

A recent study by the University of California has shown that the 'fishing policies of rich European countries are directly linked to the extinction of African animals such as elephants, monkeys and warthogs'. A 30-year study revealed that because of the depletion of fish stocks, which Ghanaians have depended on for food, people are increasingly turning to 'bushmeat' for sustenance. Between 1970 and 1998, between 16 per cent and 45 per cent of mammals in Ghana's nature reserves became locally extinct, while the European fishing of African waters grew by a factor of twenty. The mismanagement of fisheries has created a serious food crisis in Africa, which has forced more people to hunt endangered animals for food. ∎

Source: Alana Mitchell, 'Fishing Linked to Animals' Extinction', *The Globe and Mail*, 12 November 2004.

of fish are now considered threatened or endangered.[16] To make matters worse, every year 57 billion pounds (26 billion kilograms) of sealife, including fish, birds, turtles and dolphins, is unintentionally caught in nets.[17] It is estimated that 100,000 dolphins are killed this way every year.[8] The shrimp fishery is one of the most destructive because it uses trawlers, whose nets scrape along the ocean floor and destroy the habitat. A full 92 per cent of Australia's prawn catch isn't

## Kosher and halal meat

Practicing Jews and Muslims are required to eat meat that has been butchered according to specific laws. Both kosher and halal meat must come from fully conscious animals that have had their throats slit and have been completely drained of blood.

When these practices were first established thousands of years ago, they likely represented the most hygienic and humane way of killing animals. Animals had to be conscious when slaughtered to ensure that they were healthy. Their throats were to be cut with a single stroke of a very sharp knife, to ensure a quick death.[1] However now that there is a huge demand for this meat worldwide, ritual animal slaughter is no longer as humane as it was meant to be. Like most meat, the ritually slaughtered variety is also now processed at huge slaughterhouses.

However it is exempt from humane slaughter laws which require mammals to be stunned. In order to have the blood drain out, animals must be hoisted upside down in the air so that the butcher has access to the jugular vein. This puts incredible strain on the leg that the animal is lifted by, and heavy animals often suffer from broken limbs and the separation of flesh from bone. Animals are usually suspended for about 5 minutes before they are finally killed. Their heads are put in clamps to prevent them from writhing, so that the butcher is able to kill them with a single stroke.

Because these practices were meant to be as humane as possible, many Jewish and Muslim religious leaders have accepted that modern ritual slaughter needs to change. In Sweden, Norway and Switzerland, religious leaders have agreed to allow animals to be stunned before they are drained of blood. However in most other countries, ritual slaughter involves considerable pain and distress, and some therefore feel that this violates the spirit of kosher and halal laws.[2] ■

Sources; 1. Rynn Berry, *Food for the Gods* (Pythagorean, 1998). 2 Peter Singer, *Animal Liberation* 3rd edition (Pimlico, 1995).

prawn at all but other species.[17] Elliot Norse, of the Marine Conservation Biology Institute, said of the shrimp fishery: 'We're talking about destruction of marine habitat that is, if not equivalent, at least in the ballpark with clearcutting forests on land.'[18]

Animal rights groups have launched campaigns against eating fish not only because the fisheries are destroying the environment but also because fish, as vertebrates, can feel pain and distress. Drift lines and nets cause fish injuries and they can suffer for days before being hauled in. And then when the nets are brought up, the fish suffer more injuries from rapid decompression. Once on board, they usually suffocate or are crushed to death by the weight of other fish.[19]

## Factory fishing

As fish stocks decline around the world, factory fish farming has started to grow rapidly. Currently, one third of all fish consumed is farmed.[15] Like land-based livestock, fish are raised in intensive conditions. Salmon farms, for example, have anywhere up to 50,000 fish in cages. Apart from environmental concerns (massive pollution and the contamination of wild stocks), animal rights activists oppose the treatment of farmed fish, which, like cows, pigs and chickens, are fed growth hormones and antibiotics to prevent parasites, and are kept in such crowded conditions that they often get injured.[19]

They also point out that fish are often deprived of food for several days before slaughter to reduce the amount of fecal matter in the water and to make gutting less messy.[20] To make matters worse, farmed fish are usually fed wild fish – and it takes 5½ pounds (2½ kilograms) of wild caught fish to produce one pound (half a kilo) of farmed fish.[15] In fact, one third of all fish caught in the wild is used in meal to feed livestock, including farmed fish.[21]

The factory farming of any species involves a serious

disregard for animal welfare, not to mention animal rights. 'Intensively produced' food animals are ware-housed and confined, exploited to their full capacity, and then slaughtered in huge numbers. Their physical and psychological wellbeing is disregarded so that the industry can make as much money as possible from them. Activists are alarmed by the globalization of industrial farming, which has dramatically increased the number of animals exploited and worsened the conditions in which they live.

## Is there a humane alternative?

Recently 'humanely raised' meat, eggs and dairy have become more popular with consumers. In North America, a certification process has been developed in partnership with the Humane Society and the SPCA. Hormones and antibiotics are prohibited and livestock must have adequate shelter, resting areas and space to engage in natural behavior. Several animal protection organizations have endorsed the label. In addition, there are organic and free-range methods of producing meat, eggs and milk, which emphasize higher stand-ards for the care of livestock. CIWF, Canadians for the Ethical Treatment of Farm Animals and the World Society for the Protection of Animals all encourage consumers to buy animal products only from organic and free-range producers.

However, many animal rights groups warn that 'humanely-raised', organic and free-range products are not actually cruelty free. They point out that some producers place these labels on their products primarily to assuage the conscience of consumers, and actually treat their livestock only marginally better than factory-farm operators. They argue that many of these animals are also de-beaked, de-horned and castrated, and that while they may have access to the outdoors, there is no law stipulating exactly what this means. Some activists worry that the vaguely worded outdoor 'access' clause allows producers to get away with keeping their animals confined most of the time. They are particularly suspicious of free-range labeling because free-range products aren't regulated by independent certifying agencies. They worry that some so-called free-range producers are tricking consumers into purchasing products from animals that actually spend the majority of their time in cages.

Activists argue that all livestock farming, regardless of technique, is inherently cruel to animals because it ends in the animals being slaughtered. They also are quick to point out that 'humanely-raised', free-range and organic animals can be transported and slaughtered in the exact same way as factory farmed animals. Even with the more strictly regulated organic products, there are no guidelines to minimize stress during transport and slaughter. All animals suffer the horror of long truck rides without food and water and inaccuracies on the kill floor.[19,20]

Is there any way to consume animal products without directly supporting the mistreatment of livestock? Many activists say there isn't. Gene Bauston, co-founder of Farm Sanctuary, is one such person. Farm Sanctuary rescues livestock from meat, dairy and egg operations. The organization would like to see an end to all animal agriculture. Bauston suggests that people who eat animal products should go see at first hand what kind of conditions the animals live in. He believes that most people would stop eating meat, eggs and dairy if they witnessed the cruelty involved.[22] Many other animal rights organizations agree, and advocate a strict vegan diet.

**A trip to the farm**
I decided to see for myself how animals are treated at organic farms, which are the most strictly regulated of all alternative farming systems. On a cold February day, I visited Sunnivue farm, just outside London,

## Food animals

Ontario. Run by Ellinor and Alex Nurnburg and Dagmar Seiboth, the farm produces organic dairy, and some beef and eggs. It is a small operation with 65 cows (of which 25 are milked) and 27 egg-laying hens. The milk and eggs are sold through the Organic Meadow co-operative, which supplies Canada with 80 per cent of its organic dairy. Antibiotics are strictly prohibited at organic farms and all livestock must be fed organically grown grain (putting animal by-products in the feed is strictly prohibited). Having learned about the objections some animal rights activists have, even to alternative farming practices, I was curious to see how an organic farm operates.

Sunnivue is primarily a dairy operation. It uses a tethering system for its dairy cows, while the rest of the cattle roam free in large pens in the barn. During the winter months when it is well below zero, all the cows are outside for 2 hours a day and in the summer they spend at least 12 hours (sometimes all day) outside. They all go out together and are brought in twice a day for milking and feeding.

While I was at the farm, it was about 15° below zero and all the cows were inside. I was first taken to visit the calves that had been born from the dairy cows. Each dairy cow gives birth to one calf each year. As in the conventional dairy industry, all calves are taken from their mothers soon after birth because nursing cows won't allow themselves to be milked. The calves are kept in group pens with plenty of straw bedding. Ellinor tries to make sure that there's always more than one calf born at a time, so that they won't get lonely. Alex tells me that industry regulations only require that calves be fed milk for the first 20 days, but at Sunnivue all calves get natural milk for the first 120 days of their lives.

Half of the calves born on the farm are male. Most of these are raised for organic beef, but some are sold to other farms. The Nurnburgs prefer to raise their own male cows, partly because organic calves aren't worth any more than conventionally raised calves (despite the fact that they take much more time and money to produce), and also because they prefer to have control over how their animals are treated. Ellinor de-horns and castrates her male calves when they are couple of weeks old. She uses local anesthetic for de-horning and gives pain-killers for 24 hours after castration – something that is never done on intensive farms. The steers are kept on the farm until they are slaughtered at about 24 months. Sunnivue uses a small local slaughterhouse that is 40 minutes away by truck. They bring in their animals, usually just one or two at a time, in the early morning just before slaughter so they don't have to wait in the stockyard overnight.

## A cow's life

The adult dairy cows are tethered in open-concept stalls. The Nurnburgs have modified the stalls so that their cows have twice the room they would at a conventional farm, and enough room to lie down and stretch out. Each cow is given a name: because they only have a couple of dozen milking cows, the Nurnburgs are able to get to know their animals. They are familiar with the temperament and breeding history of each one. Unlike intensively-raised dairy cows, almost all Sunnivue's dairy cows retain their horns. Because they are given enough space, there isn't the fear that they will gore each other. The dairy cows are hooked up to milking machines twice a day for about an hour each time.

In the conventional dairy industry, cows are killed by the time they are about four years old. However Sunnivue doesn't routinely cull its cows and prefers to allow them to die of old age. The farm currently has milking cows that are 10 and 12 years old, and even had one cow that lived until she was 15. Not all organic dairy farms let their cows live out their natural lives, but in the Organic Meadow co-op, cows aren't usually culled until they are at least 7 years old.

Next we visited the chicken coop, which is made up of an indoor shed and an outdoor run. The chickens are provided with deep straw bedding for scratching, several perches and a nesting box. They have access outside unless it is unusually cold. The hens used to have the run of the whole farm but new regulations prohibit mixing chickens with other livestock. Ellinor expressed regret at not being able to allow the hens to roam completely freely. The chickens still have their beaks and feathers. As noted earlier, at intensive battery farms chickens have their beaks removed within days of birth and usually lose their feathers within a few weeks. Sunnivue's chickens lay about one egg every second day – this is just over half the yield of battery farms.

## A farmer's view

The animals are clean with healthy-looking coats and plumage. Intensively raised animals, on the other hand, are usually dirty because they live in crowded conditions, and are habitually stressed and sick with diarrhea. It is customary, for example, for cows in feedlots to be covered in feces. The fact that the Sunnivue's cows are so clean revealed much about their well-being. They generally seem to be healthy, relaxed, and adequately housed. None of the animals live on concrete or wire floors and all have access to fresh bedding. Waste is continually removed from the bedding.

The Nurnburgs acknowledge that not all organic animals are raised in such good conditions. They point out that not all farmers have similar facilities or the money to make improvements to their barns. Unlike in Europe, there are no government subsidies for organic farmers in Canada and the US. But they insist that the majority of organic farmers they know are committed to humane standards for their livestock, and that this is one of the major incentives for getting involved in organic farming. Ellinor, in particular, clearly feels very attached to her cows. While the cows shied away from me, they nudged and nuzzled against her. Alex explained to me that the organic farmers he knows haven't gone into it for the money. Most small organic farmers can make a comfortable living, but certainly aren't rich. Alex, Ellinor and Dagmar run their organic farm in large part because they are committed to a particular lifestyle and land ethic.

Surprisingly enough for cattle farmers, the Nurnburgs suggest that it isn't sustainable for humans to eat as much meat as they do. If food animals were not raised intensively, there simply would not be enough space to feed North Americans meat everyday. While organic livestock farming is much easier on the environment in general, it requires more land. If the 10 billion farm animals slaughtered in North America every year were given the same space as Sunnivue's livestock, farming would encroach too seriously on the planet's dwindling wilderness. The Nurnburgs suggest that people can sustainably eat meat only once or twice a week.

Ellinor readily admits that the animals raised at Sunnivue are exploited in the sense that they exist to serve human purposes, and many are eventually slaughtered. However, they are nonetheless treated with consideration during their lifetimes. The Nurnburgs make a significant effort to minimize the pain and distress of the animals they raise, even when they are destined to be eaten. This is something that cannot be said for the majority of intensive livestock operators. Farm animals would certainly be much better off if they all lived on farms like Sunnivue. Unfortunately, only five miles down the road, a new factory veal farm has recently been built – it houses three to four thousand crated veal calves in windowless sheds. This is a stark reminder that the Sunnivue animals are certainly in the minority.

However, even organically reared animals are raised to be killed and this is something that activists consider wrong. For this reason, many animal rightists believe that all husbandry is inherently unjust. Yes, animals raised organically are not abused in the same way as their intensively raised counterparts. This is mainly because livestock health and well-being is an essential component of organic farming. For this reason, many animal protection organizations actively promote organic farming practices as a more humane alternative.

However, as organic and free-range products become more popular, agri-businesses are already starting to invest in them. Companies like biotech giant Monsanto, which have proved that they have no commitment to animal welfare or the environment, have already started investing in organic foods.[23] Large corporate meat producers like ConAgra, Tyson and Cargill, and multinationals such as Kraft, General Mills and Heinz, already have significant stakes in the organic market.[24] If big business takes over organic livestock production, as it has with conventional agriculture, animal welfare will undoubtedly decline as a result. To prevent this from happening, consumers need to support independent local farmers and only buy from producers they know are personally committed to the principles of responsible stewardship.

### Small, slow steps

While global meat production is increasing and factory farming has become the standard method, animal activists have managed to secure some significant victories for farm animals in the last 30 years. Currently, many European nations are in the process of substantially reforming farm laws, so that livestock are considered under anti-cruelty laws. The European Union (EU) is currently phasing out all battery cages, sow stalls and veal crates and prohibits the use of growth hormones in livestock. Swiss law requires that all cattle have at least 90 days per year of free movement outside, that laying hens and farrowing sows have litter bedding to build nests, and that ducks have access to water for bathing. Norway has banned de-beaking and the kicking, hitting or branding of farm animals and Britain has banned forced molting (withholding food from hens so that they will immediately enter into another egg-laying cycle). The EU has also recommended that the transport of live animals be limited to 8 hours at a time. Europe is at the forefront of farm reform and improving welfare standards has broad public support. While factory farming still exists in Europe, some of its worst practices are being abolished.

Farm reform is also being adopted on a piecemeal basis in the US. Following Germany and Israel's lead, California was the first state to ban the force-feeding of geese and ducks for the production of *fois gras*. Similar bills are also being considered in Illinois, New York, and Massachusetts.

In 1995 California also passed a law preventing the transport and purchase of sick and injured mammals by stockyards and slaughterhouses. 'Downed' animals must be humanely euthanased and facilities that fail to do this can be prosecuted for cruelty. Oregon and Washington have implemented similar laws and New York is currently considering a downed animal bill. On a national level, USDA has also implemented a ban on the transport of downed cattle. In 2002, Florida set a precedent in the US by banning sow stalls and New Jersey agreed to create humane standards protocol for all farm animals.

**Humane standards**
Responding to campaigns, some of the largest fast food chains, such as McDonald's, Burger King and

## Food animals

Wendy's have agreed to implement humane standards at their slaughterhouses that exceed national guidelines (Yum Foods, which owns KFC and Taco Bell, has resisted these efforts). This is an important step because the fast food industry is one of the largest purchasers of meat products in the world. Their standards have a huge impact on industry practices. Thanks to the work of Temple Grandin, half of the mammals slaughtered in the US now go through a chute referred to in the industry as the 'highway to heaven'. Designed by Grandin, the chute encourages animals' natural herding instinct and restricts their view of the slaughter floor for the purpose of minimizing stress.[25] While animal rights activists point out that slaughter is horrible for animals even with Grandin's apparatus, its widespread adoption indicates that there is pressure on the industry, and response by parts of it, to improve animal welfare standards.

### Progress and challenges ahead

North Americans consume more meat than any other people in the world. However the public is increasingly unwilling to purchase products associated with cruelty. Veal production dropped by 60 per cent in the 1980s after the animal movement campaigned to educate the public about the way veal calves are raised.[8] Currently about 6 per cent of Americans have opted for a vegetarian diet and doctors have observed that vegetarianism is particularly common among young people.[26] In Canada, 8 per cent of teens aged 15-18 are vegetarian.[27] This trend suggests that North American consumption patterns may change quite dramatically in the future. McDonald's, Burger King and Harvey's have put vegetarian burgers on their menus and most restaurants in North America now carry vegetarian options: 15 years ago, this was unheard of.

Despite the progress that has been made, animal

activists believe that the campaign against the industrial exploitation of food animals is now more important than ever. Faced with increasing public condemnation in the West, many agribusinesses are moving their operations to the Global South where there are usually less rigid environmental and animal welfare laws in place. Critics fear that unless international efforts are made to preserve traditional farming, intensive livestock will become the dominant form of production around the world.

**1** Eric Schlosser, *Fast Food Nation* (Perennial, 2001). **2** Quoted in Annabelle Sabloff, *Reordering the Natural World* (University of Toronto Press, 2001). **3** Tom Regan, *Empty Cages* (Rowman & Littlefield, 2004). **4** Grace Factory Farm Project, www.factoryfarming.org **5** Animal Aid, www.animalaid.org.uk **6** Canadians for Ethical Treatment of Food Animals, www.cetfa.com **7** Stephanie Brown and John Youngman, 'The Disgraceful Secret Down on the Farm', *Vancouver Sun*, 3 November 2003. **8** Peter Singer, *Animal Liberation*, 3$^{rd}$ edition (Pimlico, 1995). **9** Quoted in 'Factory Farms Grow New Roots in Developing World', *Environment News Service*, April 2003 (22). **10** 'Humans and other animals – the facts', *New Internationalist* No 215, January 1991. **11** *The Independent*, 18 November 2003. **12** Darrin Qualman and Nettie Wiebe, 'The Structural Adjustment of Canadian Agriculture', Canadian Centre for Policy Alternatives. **13** Global Action Network, *Animal Transport* (pamphlet). **14** Charlotte Montgomery, *Blood Relations* (Between the Lines, 2000). **15** 'Fishing – the facts', *New Internationalist* No 325, July 2000. **16** Steve Lustgarden, 'Fish: What's the Catch', www.eathsave.org **17** Tom Knudson, 'Waste on Grand Scale Loots Sea', Sacramento Bee, 1995, www.sacbee.com **18** Quoted in Janet Raloff, 'Fishing for Answers', *Science News* 150, October, 1996. **19** People for the Ethical Treatment of Animals, www.peta.org **20** Farm Sanctuary, www.farmsanctuary.org **21** Carl Safina, 'The World's Imperiled Fish', *Scientific American*, November 1995. **22** Gene Bauston, Q&A at screening of *Peaceble Kingdom* (Toronto, 2004). **23** Harold Brown, 'What's Wrong with Free-Range and Organic', lecture at Toronto Animal Rights Society, 2005. **24** 'Karma Co-op', *The Chronicle*, December 2005. **25** Matthew Scully, *Dominion* (St Martin's Press, 2002). **26** *The New York Times*, 23 July 2000. **27** *The Globe and Mail*, 2 February 2005.

# 4 Animal entertainers

*'From infants to the aged, regardless of gender, people appear to be irresistibly drawn into intimate contact with [animals].'*

– Annabelle Sabloff,
Reordering the Natural World[1]

**Almost everywhere you turn in society, animals are forced to provide 'amusement' for humans. Circuses, hunting, racing and many other forms of 'entertainment' often cause animals tremendous suffering.**

HUMANS ARE DEEPLY fascinated with animals and have been interacting with them for millennia. Prehistoric humans tamed and trained dogs for hunting and companionship and the ancient Egyptians domesticated cats, which they revered as divine creatures. For entertainment, the Romans watched people fight animals in their coliseums. Bear and bull baiting and dog and cock fighting began to be widely practiced in the Middle Ages. Today, humans continue to demonstrate the desire to get face to face with animals, in order to observe them, nurture them, and even compete with them.

Most children are delighted to go to zoos and aquariums, ride elephants at the circus, and visit pet stores. Many adults also feel this delight and want to expose their children to the experience. Because so many people in developed nations have little contact with the natural world, they seek to connect with animals in manufactured settings. Even recreational hunters feel that through the act of killing, they are actually communing with animals.

While people have always sought out connection with animals, over the last century animal entertainment and companionship have become multi-billion dollar global industries. Literally billions of animals are used for entertainment and companionship around the world. Activists are concerned that even the most seemingly benign uses of animals for human pleasure are seriously detrimental to the creatures involved.

## Hunting

Sport hunting is a widespread pastime, particularly in North America. In the US, about $21 billion is spent every year on hunting supplies, and 134 million animals are killed.[2] In Canada, recreational hunting is also widespread; in British Columbia alone, hunters spend $100 million a year.[3] In Europe hunting is less common because there is less wilderness and wildlife available. However, the practice of hunting with dogs in agricultural areas remains popular, particularly among the British upper classes. Even animal welfare proponents, who do not believe that animals possess fundamental rights, acknowledge that sport hunting is incredibly cruel and lobby against it in all its forms.

The vast majority of hunting in North America and Europe is not done to procure food or valuable animal pelts, but for recreational purposes. The 'thrill of the chase' and mounted trophies are the main incentives. Hunters often use sophisticated technology to catch their prey; electronic and heat-seeking tracking devices, high-powered scopes, night vision goggles and all-terrain vehicles significantly decrease the odds for the animals.[4] Hunters also lure their prey with food when they are coming out of hibernation using calling devices, and 'musks' (often deer urine).

While more lethal, these high-tech methods perhaps end up being more 'humane' than traditional hunting methods. Hunters who use traditional methods are not necessarily skilled enough to actually capture their prey. For example, while rifle bullets tend to kill animals quickly because of high impact, arrowheads can cause animals to hemorrhage to death.[4] In this way, for every animal killed quickly by a bow-hunter, one escapes and is left to die slowly.[5]

One serious concern is the hunting of endangered or threatened species. Some European and North American hunters travel to Africa and Asia where they can hunt big game. According to the League Against Cruel Sports, in parts of South Africa trophy hunting represents a substantial portion of tourism revenue. Between 1996 and 2002, European hunters killed 3,812 African elephants, 2,623 leopards, 2,006 baboons and 539 cheetahs.[6] All but baboons are considered threatened species.

During the same period, European hunters also traveled to Canada to kill 2,119 grizzly bears, also endangered. Yet this represents only a small fraction of the number of grizzlies killed because 80 per cent of the foreign bear hunters visiting British Colombia are American.[7] Both animal rights activists and conservationists are worried about this phenomenon because so many animals have been hunted to extinction over the past hundred years, and more and more species become endangered each day. However AR activists are as opposed to the hunting of common animals as they are to the hunting of endangered ones because common animals are just as capable of suffering.

'Canned hunts' are becoming increasingly popular for those who want to experience killing an animal without actually acquiring any hunting skills. Hunt ranches breed animals in captivity for hunters to shoot. Some breed exotic animals (often 'surplus' animals purchased from zoos)[2]; others prefer to raise hunting 'favorites', like deer and elk. Hunt ranches are of particular concern for animal rights activists because in them, animals have no possible chance of escape. The animals, lacking wild instincts and kept in fenced enclosures, are incredibly easy targets because they are not afraid of humans. Farmed wild animals are also susceptible to illness when kept in captivity. When epidemics break out on hunt ranches, entire herds are exterminated and diseases spread to local livestock and wild populations.[3] Even many hunters find hunt ranches repugnant because they promote the easy killing of domesticated animals. Nevertheless, 'canned hunting' is well established in the US and Europe and is starting to make inroads in Canada as well.

Many hunters equate the freedom to hunt with freedom of religion and believe that hunting should be a government-protected right.[4] The hunting lobby has significant influence with governments in many countries and is generally consulted about conservation and wildlife regulations.

## Bullfighting

Although illegal in Canada, the US and Britain, bullfighting is common in Spain, Portugal, France and parts of Latin America. Proponents of the sport claim that it is an important tradition that should be preserved. However, studies demonstrate that most of those attending are not locals, but tourists from abroad. For example, a Gallup poll showed that 69 per cent of Spaniards have no interest in going to bullfights. PETA argues that it is primarily American tourists that keep the practice alive and that the tourism industry is therefore one of the biggest supporters of the sport.[8]

Bullfighting is a slow and painful process. Bulls are first chased and taunted by men on horseback, known as *picadors*. Matadors then repeatedly stab the bulls with *banderillas* (which have a 2-inch metal spike and barb at the end) until they become exhausted and collapse. They are then slaughtered in the arena or dragged out by a truck and slaughtered later. Sometimes, the ears and tail are cut off and presented as a gift of honor to the matador. The bull may still be alive when this happens. Because bullfighting is a profitable spectacle and popular matadors are expected to perform well, about 20 per cent of all bulls are illegally drugged or dehydrated with Epsom salts so that they are easier to defeat. Another common procedure is to rub petroleum jelly on the bull's eyes to diminish its sight. Bulls aren't the only victims of bullfighting; approximately 200 horses a year are also gored and die. Because some *picadors* blindfold their horses, they are not always able to maneuver away from the charging bull.[8]

Many organizations are lobbying to put an end to the sport. There have been mass protests and petitioning campaigns throughout Spain and several municipalities have now either banned or condemned bullfighting.

### Rodeo

The rodeo is an extremely popular event in North America. Because of the frontier tradition and myths about cowboys, ranchers and farmers, the American and Canadian public feels that the rodeo reflects their roots. In the US alone, 25 million people attend such events every year.[2] However it's clear that most rodeos involve considerable discomfort and even pain for the animals involved. In many ways, the rodeo is a form of blood sport. However, according to the Humane Society in Calgary (the city which is home to the multi-million dollar annual Calgary Stampede), the public isn't very interested in reforming rodeo events. Despite the fact that traditional ranchers would never allow people to taunt and abuse their valuable animals for fun, people somehow seem to associate what happens at the rodeo with time-honored traditions. Take calf-roping for example: back in the day this was never done for entertainment, but when ranchers needed to bring in sick calves to get veterinary treatment.[3]

In modern day rodeos, tame horses and bulls are sometimes given electric shocks to get them 'bucking' or have straps squeezed around their lower abdomens to put pressure on their groin areas. Apart from this kind of discomfort, animals are sometimes seriously injured and even killed at the rodeo. A USDA meat inspector said that the rodeo horses and cows that come to slaughterhouses are so terribly bruised that there are few places were the skin is actually attached to the muscle. Animals also commonly have broken ribs and punctured lungs.[2] For these reasons, animal rights activists believe that the rodeo is nothing but socially sanctioned animal abuse.

## Horse and dog racing

Horse and dog racing have been popular betting sports for hundreds of years. Every year, billions of dollars are placed on bets worldwide. On first thought, it seems perfectly natural for a horse or dog to run. However, the racing industry systematically exploits and kills animals that humans have historically bonded with.

Professional racing is incredibly hard on horses and dogs because they are expected to run in short, fast bursts which is contrary to what they would do in nature. When they are not racing, they are confined to stables and kennels and not permitted to move at all. Racehorses often are stabled for 20 hours a day[6] and greyhounds are crated (in crates as small as 3 feet by 3 feet) for up to 22 hours a day.[2] This can lead to serious medical problems. Both racehorses and greyhounds suffer from bone damage due to lack of exercise and the stress of running on tracks. In addition, 55 per cent of racehorses suffer from bleeding lungs and 100 per cent from ulcerated stomachs.[6] Greyhounds commonly suffer from tick-borne diseases, parasites and giardia. An average of 30 per cent of all race dogs are on sick/injured lists at any given time.[9]

Because a winning animal can make so much money, trainers do whatever they can to maximize performance. Racehorses are often medically 'altered' to make them run faster. 'Tubing' and 'pinfiring' are common practices.

The first involves the insertion of a metal tube into the horse's neck to allow increased air intake into the lungs; the second involves the insertion of hot needles into injured tendons/ligaments to stimulate inflammation, ie creating a cushion of fluid so that the horse can run while injured.[6] Female greyhounds are continually administered anabolic steroids (methyl testosterone) to prevent menstruation. Both horses and dogs are routinely given pain medication so that they can race while injured.

Every year in the US, 20,000 greyhounds are destroyed. These are animals that are sick, injured or too slow to win races.[10] In the UK, about 10,000 grey-hounds are killed annually.[11] While some make it to shelters, the dogs that aren't killed directly are often donated to laboratories for scientific research. For example, between 1995-8, Colorado State University alone had 2,650 greyhounds donated for research.[2]

### Horses for courses

Horses are even more expensive to care for, and so those not fast enough for the racetrack are also disposed of. There are about 640,000 race horses registered in the US. However even successful race-horses only have a career of about 3 years (and a 30-year life span). Several thousand a year are slaughtered for human and petfood consumption. In addition, tens of thousands of thoroughbred foals (35,000 a year in the US, and 15,000 a year in the UK) are born in the racing industry each year. Like domestic food animals, they are raised intensively and considered a 'crop'. Less than half of the foals born every year actu-ally make it to the racetrack because they aren't fast enough. There are too many to be placed in adoptive homes or shelters, and so the majority of these 'rejects' inevitably end up as food as well.

## Circuses

The circus is an event that people often equate with quality family time and wholesome fun. However, activists believe that the animal acts in circuses are cruel. Wild animals in circuses are denied their most basic need – space. In the wild, lions have a natural range of 8-156 square miles; Indian tigers have a range of 8-60 square miles; and elephants a range of 5-1,350 square miles. Ringling Brothers, one the biggest animal circuses, provides 36-foot cages for groups of seven to nine big cats.[2] However other circuses use cages as small as 4 x 8 feet for individual animals.[12] Elephants are sometimes chained by two legs with enough slack to allow them to take a step or two and lie down. Others are kept in electrically fenced compounds (which allow only slightly more movement). Wild animals require sufficient space to remain physically and psychologically healthy. Even the best equipped circuses are not able to provide them with this.

Circuses often travel across countries and continents and even around the world. It is standard for a circus to be on the road for 40-50 weeks every year, which means that the animals spend most of their lives caged and in transport vehicles that are often unheated and poorly ventilated.

Circus animals are required to do tricks that they would never perform in the wild. In order to compel animals to do their tricks, trainers use bullhooks, whips and electric prods. Trainers use fear, pain and threat of punishment to get tigers to leap through rings of fire, elephants to do handstands and bears to ride bicycles. Circus animals often develop serious mental illnesses as a result of this treatment and have been known to turn on their trainers and to self-mutilate.

To make matters worse there have been dozens of reports of 'widespread, systematic abuse' of animals in circuses.[12] At least 19 elephants with Ringling

## Animal entertainers

Brothers have died since 1992. One 8-month old elephant was euthanized when he fractured his two hind legs from doing tricks. Another was euthanized because he had osteoarthritis standing on concrete 23 hours a day. Yet another died from drowning in a pond when he tried to escape a beating from his trainer.

In 1999, a USDA inspector found two baby elephants with serious lesions and scarring from being chained to forcibly separate them from their mothers.[8] Ringling Brothers has 'more than 100 times... been cited by USDA for deficiencies in animals' care'. And in 1998, 'the circus paid $20,000 to settle USDA charges of 'failing to provide veterinary care to a dying baby elephant.'[13]

Because death, injury and severe deprivation are standard in circuses that use animals, both welfare and AR groups are working hard to ban such acts from traveling circuses. Some circuses share this view. Pierre Parisien, artistic director of the *Cirque du Soleil*, said, 'We will never have animals in our shows. They are animals, not performers, they should be in the wild.'

## Marine parks

In many ways, marine parks are similar to circuses. While some claim to fulfil a conservation and educational role, the majority are primarily entertainment facilities because their main attraction is dolphin and orca shows.[14] Like circus animals, dolphins and orcas

---

**Circus acts**
**Countries that have banned circus animal acts:**
Austria, Costa Rica, Denmark, Finland, India, Norway, Singapore, Sweden, Switzerland
**Countries where animal acts are banned in some states/provinces and municipalities:**
Australia, Brazil, Canada, Venezuela, UK (over 200 municipalities), US.

are kept in very small spaces. In nature, dolphins swim about 25 miles a day, and orcas swim up to 100 miles a day. However, in marine parks these creatures are kept in tanks as small as 24 x 24 feet square and 6 feet deep.[2] It takes only a few seconds to swim from one end of the tank to the other. Almost all whales in captivity have collapsed dorsal fins because they are forced to spend so much time on the surface.[8] Another problem is that the sound waves that cetaceans use to communicate and navigate bounce off the walls of their tanks, creating 'a meaningless jumble of noise, confusing and disorientating them'.[15] One expert has likened this to the human experience of living in a mirrored room.[14]

Tanks are often kept chlorinated to decrease bacteria content – especially 'petting' tanks where the cetaceans are repeatedly touched by visitors to the aquarium. The chlorine can cause serious eye and skin irritation and even blindness.[14] Florida's Ocean World was closed down because excessive chlorination had caused dolphins' skin to peel off.[8]

Like circus animals, dolphins and whales in captivity are expected to perform. While many of the acts they do look like 'fun', they are motivated by food. While giving animals food for tricks may seem like positive reinforcement, it is nonetheless a method for forcing them to do things they would never do of their own volition. Some marine parks even withhold food from dolphins and orcas before performances.[8]

The transition from the wild to captivity is extremely traumatizing to cetaceans. Some need to be kept in complete isolation because of behavioral issues. Yet isolation in tanks and separation from others, is, in the words of a former trainer, 'psychological torture'. Whales and dolphins in captivity commonly become psychologically damaged – they stop vocalizing, swim in endless circles, become depressed, are aggressive toward humans, and have even been known to try to kill themselves.[14] Not only are captive whales and dolphins unhappy, they are also unhealthy. In the wild, orcas live to over 50 years; in captivity they only survive roughly 10 years. Dolphins have a natural life span of 25 years, but rarely survive 6 years in captivity. Over 50 per cent of dolphins die within the first 2 years of captivity.[8]

A growing number of scientists believes that whales and dolphins currently in captivity can and should be rehabilitated and released. Some countries are starting to realize the inherent cruelty of capturing cetaceans for captivity and have banned marine exhibits. Both animal rights, and animal welfare, advocates are adamantly opposed to keeping these highly intelligent and social animals in captivity.

## Zoos
Zoos were first established in Britain in the early 19th century. The earliest ones were very much a symbol of human dominance of nature (and in particular, of Britain's domination over its colonies).[16] Today, there are 10,000 zoos worldwide with more than 100 million visitors every year.[17] However, the emphasis has changed drastically since zoos were first started. They now emphasize their educational and conservationist, as opposed to entertainment, roles.

Zoos are extremely controversial within the animal protection movement. While some conservationists insist that captive breeding programs are essential to the preservation of some species, others argue that zoos' main incentive really is profit.

They point out that of the 6,000 species that are classified as threatened or endangered, only 120 are in captive breeding programs and only 16 species have been successfully reintroduced into the wild (mostly birds).[18] First of all, many animals don't breed successfully in captivity. Secondly, zoo animals are rarely equipped to survive in the wild – often they fail to develop the necessary skills and have little resistance to common diseases.

For these reasons, and because natural habitat is dwindling, many breeding programs don't actually ever release their animals.[17] However, precisely because captive breeding programs have been the major justification for zoos in the last 15 years, most zoos retain them regardless of whether they are successful or not.[19] Some critics argue that the billions of dollars spent on zoos would be better spent protecting animals in the wild. For example, the annual operating costs of Garamba National Park in the Democratic Republic of Congo, which protects thousands of animals, is the same as the annual cost for the upkeep of 16 rhinos in a typical zoo.[19] If money spent on captive breeding were put into habitat protection, endangered species would have a much better chance of surviving in the long term.

AR and welfare activists have also seriously criticized conditions in even the best zoos. Behind the scenes, most cells for animals are made of barren concrete and tile. Exhibition areas may appear to be stimulating, but lack privacy and only represent a tiny fraction of the space an animal would inhabit in the wild. Flooring is often inappropriate which leads to foot and bone abnormalities. Adequate heat, shade, or ventilation is rarely provided.

## Psychologically damaged
Many animals kept in zoos, like those in circuses and aquariums, are psychologically damaged through boredom, lack of social interaction, and lack of space. Animals with large natural ranges and complex social structures are particularly likely to suffer. For example, elephants in zoos are usually kept in pairs; however, in the wild, they would likely encounter around 250 other elephants and have intimate relationships with herd members.[19] They do not naturally breed until

they are 18-20 years old, but are often bred in captive breeding programs as early as 12 years of age. For this reason, young captive mothers often reject their calves because they are too young and do not have the support of the herd as they would naturally.[20]

Similarly, polar bears suffer tremendously in captivity. In their natural habitat they have a 20-30,000 square kilometer range; in zoos they live in pens. They are also prone to overheating because they have hollow hair shafts and black skin to attract heat. In zoos in southern climates, polar bears sometimes turn green because algae grow in their hair shafts. Polar bears in zoos have been observed engaging in stereotypic repetitive motions and even self-mutilation.[19] One survey conducted in the UK in 1985 found that about 60 per cent of polar bears in British zoos were psychotic.[16]

Activists balk at many of the standard practices in zoos. They point out that the majority of such places are not regulated or certified; substandard 'roadside' zoos far outnumber respected establishments. Yet even in well-funded ones, animals are still expected to entertain the public and in some cases even perform tricks. It is also routine to cull 'surplus' creatures when there isn't enough space, or the animals have ceased to attract the public. In addition, zoos continue to capture animals in the wild when breeding programs fail.

However, AR activists also offer a much deeper criticism of zoos. They argue that it is fundamentally cruel to keep a wild animal in captivity whether or not it will help protect an endangered species or educate the public. They suggest that zoo life destroys a creature's basic right to behave naturally, interact socially, and make day-to-day choices. For this reason, they believe that keeping any animal in a zoo is inherently wrong because it serves our interests rather than those of the individual animal.[16] They argue that conservation in the wild and habitat protection are the only ethical ways to protect endangered animals.

## Pets

Pets are now a big business.[16] After sport hunting, pet ownership is the next largest industry involving animals for entertainment. In the richer Western countries, people spend a great deal of money acquiring and caring for their pets. In consequence, pet stores, breeders, and pet food manufacturers make massive profits. The international exotic pet trade, one quarter of which is illegal, is one of the most lucrative branches of the pet industry. Americans alone spend $15 billion a year purchasing exotic pets.[21]

When animal rights are taken to their logical conclusion, pet ownership is also a form of animal exploitation. As one activist has pointed out: 'We feed emotionally on dog, cat or budgerigar, just as assuredly as we feed bodily on chicken, pig and bullock.'[16] We use pets for our own pleasure – they offer us companionship, comfort, and even security. Even the most benign pet owners expect certain standards from their pets and make efforts to minimize their pets' animal natures.[1] Some pet owners routinely de-claw, de-bark, crop the tails and clip the wings of their pets. They also attempt to 'deodorize' their pets with shampoos and colognes and discourage so-called 'destructive' habits, like scratching, chewing, or marking territory. When pets do not conform to their owners' expectations they are scolded, punished or even abandoned. Some activists believe that even pets that are loved and treated well are essentially slaves to humans.

One of the biggest problems is that the wellbeing of pets 'rests entirely on the goodwill of humans'.[3] Millions of pets are abused and neglected every year. In one Canadian province alone, there were over 15,000 reports of animal cruelty in 1998. But studies show that only about 1 per cent of cruelty cases are actually reported.[3] A far bigger problem is the huge numbers of pet owners who abandon their animals.

In the US, which has the largest number of pets in the world, 20-30 million cats and dogs are destroyed every year after being discarded by their owners. Many people think that they are being humane by bringing their unwanted pets to shelters.

However shelter life for most animals is incredibly unhappy. Animals are terrified, lonely and bored. Some, particularly dogs, become so disturbed from being caged that they become too dangerous to be adopted. Diseases run rampant in shelter environments and lack of funds makes it hard for overworked staff to keep up. And because so many pets are surrendered every day, many shelters are forced to euthanase the animals that aren't adopted quickly. Some even sell unwanted cats and dogs to laboratories. In Canada, where no laws exist to regulate this practice, over 5,000 lost and abandoned pets are used in experiments every year.[22]

### Breeding pets

Despite the pet overpopulation crisis, breeders continue to produce animals for pet stores and private buyers. While some small breeders are extremely committed to welfare standards, many breeding facilities are little better than factory farms. Animals are confined in small, often dirty crates and are denied freedom of movement or attention. They are also denied proper exercise and socialization. Females are bred until they are 'spent' and then they are destroyed. Most pure-bred pets have genetic defects – many are predisposed to heart and organ weakness, aggression, bad bones and joints, and even cancer. These ailments are the side effects of selective breeding practices. Some pure-bred varieties also are mutilated to adhere to breed standards. Many breeds of dogs have their ears and tails cropped without anesthetic. While kittens and puppies born in large breeding facilities sometimes survive long enough to make it to pet stores, birds, reptiles and other small animals often die because they are shipped before they are properly weaned. Some of the breeders that supply pet stores also supply laboratories that conduct experiments on animals.[8]

The animals that make it as far as pet stores are not guaranteed safety. Often basic anti-cruelty laws are violated, especially in large pet store chains with poorly trained staff. Animals here are sometimes deprived of their most basic needs – proper food, water and housing. Lizards and baby birds often die because they are fed the wrong diet or aren't kept warm enough. Adult birds become psychotic because they are confined to tiny cages without any stimulation. And mice often live in cages that are overcrowded and full of corpses.[8]

The exotic pet trade is particularly hard on animals. Some exotics are bred in conditions similar to those described above, but the majority are caught from the wild, often illegally. In some parts of the world, the illegal pet trade has led to local species extinction.[23] Exotic pets are stunned or trapped and then removed from their natural and social environment. Trappers routinely kill mother animals in order to catch their babies for the trade. Some studies estimate that for every animal taken live, ten others are killed in the attempt.[24] Captured birds, fish and reptiles are

## The tropical fish trade

Every year millions of tropical fish are captured for aquarium owners and collectors. One common method used is to spray clouds of cyanide around coral reefs, where the fish live. The dazed fish come out of the coral to escape the poison. Up top 90 per cent of these fish die or are injured.

Many of those that survive long enough to be shipped die soon after reaching their destination because they have damaged stomachs and intestines. The use of cyanide also permanently damages coral reefs, and fishers in Southeast Asia and the Pacific have noted a drastic decline in fish stocks because of this. ■

Source: Anouk Ride, 'Dead in the Water', *New Internationalist* No 325, July 2000.

particularly vulnerable during the long trip to Europe and North America and many do not survive. Around 40-50 per cent of the finches and waxbills that are captured in Senegal die before being successfully exported.[21]

While it is illegal to catch many species from the wild, it is legal to own any animal that has been bred in captivity. For example, it is legal to buy an animal that is endangered in the wild – such as a tiger – from a zoo or breeder. Currently 10,000 tigers are owned as pets in North America – often kept in the backyard. They can be bought for as little as $50.[19]

Experts believe that because exotic pets have not been domesticated to some degree, they never become entirely tame or comfortable in captivity. For this reason, it is cruel to keep them confined to small spaces and isolated from other members of their species. Cockatoos and macaws, two of the most common breeds of exotic birds kept as pets, will self-mutilate and methodically pull out their feathers when they are lonely or have lost their mate.[3] Exotics are forced to live in a climate and environment that is completely unsuited to their habits and needs. The transition is so difficult that 90 per cent of reptiles die within their first year of captivity.[21]

It is almost impossible to keep an exotic pet healthy and stimulated. Because they are difficult to care for and can become very large, they are often abandoned. Unwanted reptiles and snakes are simply 'let go' into the community. Some die from exposure or starvation; the lucky ones end up at shelters and sanctuaries. Many of the people involved in exotic pet rescue believe that it is wrong to own such animals and that it should be illegal for pet stores to sell them.[3]

## Pet food

The pet food industry also directly harms animals. Most companies conduct the same experiments on animals as other industries, in order to gauge the safety and efficiency of their products. In a recently publicized exposé on Iams pet food, it was revealed that laboratory animals are abused at Iams's research facilities. While the company maintains that it doesn't perform lethal tests on animals, it performs painful non-lethal experiments (for example, cutting flesh out of dogs' thighs to test muscle mass). Iams's lab animals are allegedly also severely neglected. They are kept in small, barren cages in windowless buildings. Some cages are filthy with excrement and sometimes so poorly designed they are dangerous. A PETA investigation found that the majority of Iams's lab animals were in poor physical condition and were nearly psychotic from lack of exercise and stimulation.[8]

Pet food is generally made from slaughterhouse refuse. This means that it comes from dead, dying, diseased, or disabled animals that are unfit for human consumption ('downed' animals), or from 'byproducts' such as blood, bones, brains, organs, skin and so on. Our pets mostly eat animals that are considered a threat to human health because of potential diseases and infections. For this reason, pet food is heated to extreme temperatures to kill germs. If 'downed' animals couldn't be sold as pet food – which is a multi-billion dollar industry – meat producers would have an incentive to take better care of their livestock and ensure their safety during transport. As it stands, when we buy food for our pets, we are contributing to the worst excesses of factory farming. Because of this, some animal rights groups advocate vegetarian diets for pets (see chapter 9 for alternatives).

It is entirely legal to make cat and dog food out of rendered cats and dogs. One Canadian company put 40,000 pounds of dead pets into its pet food every week, until it voluntarily gave up the practice in 2001.[25] Most of the dead pets used in pet food are procured from shelters that destroy animals they don't have room for. The lessons learned from 'mad cow' disease have not affected laws regarding pet food.

## To have a pet, or not

Not all animal rights activists oppose pet ownership in principle, because some domesticated animals, particularly dogs and cats, often thrive as companion animals and show no desire to leave their owners.[17] Even those who do oppose the idea of pets believe that it is our responsibility to care for those that already exist. However, almost all animal rights groups have serious problems with how the pet industry functions. The world's largest AR organization, PETA, encourages people not to acquire exotic pets, fish, and caged birds and rodents. It argues that these forms of pet ownership are inherently cruel because they remove animals from their natural environment and keep them isolated from other members of their species. PETA also urges animal lovers to buy only from shelters and never from pet stores or breeders, so that the pets that already exist will get homes and more won't be bred.

One interesting and potentially contradictory position adopted by AR groups regards spaying and neutering. While one could argue that this practice violates pets' individual rights, almost all animal rights groups actively promote it. They argue that pets should be neutered to prevent the potential suffering of their offspring. Because there is such an overpopulation of dogs and cats, animal activists are willing to compromise on individual rights for the future wellbeing of the species (something many are not willing to do when it comes to endangered species in the wild).

## Changing attitudes

Some countries are also starting to question the ethics of animal sports and entertainment. The British Government, for example, recently banned hunting

## TV and film

Despite advances in digital technology that allow the realistic replication of animals using computer images, the use of animals in film and television is still widespread. Many directors believe that digital imaging looks fake and it is still slightly cheaper to use the real thing rather than create high-quality computer animation. In order to fulfill the demand for animal 'actors' there are hundreds of rental agencies that supply for film and television production. Producers can choose from an array of insects and reptiles, and trained cats, dogs, horses, wildlife and primates. While many countries have laws that protect animals from physical harm while on the set, the conditions in which animals are housed and transported are not regulated. Insects, snakes and rodents are routinely kept in small boxes. The use of chimpanzees has provoked particular criticism from the AR community because only juveniles can be safely handled. Once chimpanzees mature, they become strong and unmanageable and need to be retired. They often end up abandoned in zoos and even donated to laboratories.[1]

Many people learn what they know about animals through film and TV. The way they are represented has a huge impact on how humans understand the animal kingdom. Some films and TV shows still depict them behaving like humans – talking, walking on two legs, wearing clothes, having human thoughts and motivations. This creates unrealistic stereotypes about ways animals should act and leads to widespread misconceptions about animals' natural behaviors.[2] ∎

Sources: 1 www.nomoremonkeybusiness.com 2 Annabelle Sabloff, *Reordering the Natural World*, Toronto, 2001.

with dogs, so outlawing the popular form of fox-hunting and also hare coursing. These sports have been popular in Britain for centuries, and still are with Britain's landed élite. While many hunting groups have threatened to break the law and continue their sport, most people back the ban.

The plight of sea mammals in captivity has also provoked government action. Brazil has outlawed all marine displays, Israel has stopped the importation of dolphins, and Canada has prohibited the capture of beluga whales. South Carolina is the first US state to ban marine acts, but other states are also considering doing so. In the UK, no government regulation was needed – a public boycott forced all marine parks to close. Many countries, such as India, have banned wild animal acts altogether. Around 200 municipalities in the UK, 33 in Canada and 27 in the US have also banned animal circus acts.

Fortunately, zoos are starting to recognize that captivity can be cruel for some animals. Several institutions in Canada and the US (in Vancouver, San Francisco and Detroit) have ended their endangered elephant exhibits because they recognize that elephants, who are highly intelligent, do not do well in captivity, and often die prematurely.[26] This is an encouraging start for activists who hope that the zoo staff will begin to accept how traumatizing captivity is for all wild animals.

The EU has made serious efforts to reform cruelty statutes to protect pets under the law. The European Convention for the Protection of Pets prohibits the infliction of unnecessary pain and suffering on companion animals, the abandonment of pets, or the possession of those unsuited to captivity. The trend in European law is to move away from the notion of pets as merely property and acknowledge their inherent value. For example, Austria has banned the outdoor chaining of dogs and Switzerland has rules regarding access to fresh air and exercise. New Zealand/Aotearoa has banned the cropping of a pet's ears, as well as the pin-firing of horses. Australia has banned the de-clawing of cats.

The US on the other hand has no federal law that protects companion animals. However, the trend in state laws has moved toward stricter penalties for animal cruelty and currently 41 states consider some forms of animal cruelty felony crimes (as opposed to misdemeanors). Unfortunately, most American animal cruelty laws (as well as Canadian laws) emphasize the rights of pet owners as opposed to the rights of the animals, and consider pets valuable only as property.

Colorado is the first state to amend its cruelty laws to acknowledge the moral value of such animals.[27]

While these are significant victories, progressive laws only affect a small number of animals used worldwide for entertainment. Millions of wild and domesticated ones are nonetheless killed, abused and neglected for the sake of human amusement. Luckily, because these animals used are often very visible to the public, efforts are being made in almost every country in the world to alleviate their suffering.

**1** Annabelle Sabloff, *Reordering the Natural World* (University of Toronto Press, 2001). **2** Tom Regan, *Empty Cages*, (Rowman & Littlefield, 2004). **3** Charlotte Montgomery, *Blood Relations* (Between the Lines, 2000). **4** *Outdoors Canada*, October 2004. **5** Animal Protection Institute, www.api4animals.org **6** League Against Cruel Sports, www.league.uk.com; Animal Aid, www.animalaid.org.uk **7** *Boston Herald*, 21 May 2004. **8** People for the Ethical Treatment of Animals, www.peta.org **9** Greyhound Protection League, www.greyhounds.org **10** National Humane Education Society, www.nhes.org **11** League Against Cruel Sports, www.league.uk.com **12** Zoocheck, www.zoocheck.com **13** Richard Ouzounian, 'Latest Act For Circus is Modernizing', *Toronto Star*, 10 November 2004. **14** Rob Laidlaw, 'Dolphins and Whales in Captivity: Is it justified?', www.zoocheck.com **15** Niagara Action for Animals, 'Freedom vs. Captivity', (pamphlet). **16** Robert Garner, *Animals, Politics and Morality* (Manchester University Press, 1993). **17** Lewis Petrinovich, *Darwinian Dominion*, (MIT Press, 1999). **18** Advocates for Animals, www.advocatesforanimals.org.uk **19** Rob Laidlaw, 'Nature in a Box', lecture at Toronto Animals Rights Society, 2004 **20** *Globe and Mail*, 9 December 2004. **21** Humane Society of the United States, www.hsus.org **22** Animal Alliance of Canada, 'Pound Seizure – Pets in Experimentation', (pamphlet). **23** World Society for the Protection of Animals, www.wspa-international.org **24** Tom Regan, *All That Dwell Therein* (University of California Press, 1982). **25** Eric Schlosser, *Fast Food Nation*, (Perennial, 2002). **26** *Globe and Mail*, 19 November 2004; *Globe and Mail*, 26 July 2004. **27** Paige Tomaselli, 'International Comparative Animal Cruelty Laws', www.animallaw.info

# 5 Animals and 'progress'

*'Vivisection is a social evil because if it advances human knowledge, it does so at the expense of human character.'*

– GEORGE BERNARD SHAW
(1856-1950), PLAYWRIGHT

**Animals and the natural world have long borne the brunt of the human pursuit of 'progress'. Despite viable humane alternatives, animal testing and vivisection continue to be a common but largely unnecessary facet of modern scientific research.**

PEOPLE TEND TO take it for granted that 'progress' is beneficial. Western culture presumes that scientific innovation and economic expansion are always positive things that improve human lives. But as Ronald Wright, author of a *A Short History of Progress*, has shown, progress can be a trap. Not only has it caused massive human suffering – particularly to indigenous cultures, citizens of developing nations and the working poor – but it has been even more devastating for the planet and the animals that inhabit it. Ultimately the natural world has borne the brunt of human 'progress'.

We 'are serial killers beyond reason': we kill huge quantities of plants and animals because we use the planet's resources so carelessly.[1] The leading cause of unintentional animal suffering is industrial, agricultural, urban and resource development. As the human population grows and wealthy nations consume more and more, we use an increasingly large proportion of the earth's surface to survive. We build towns, cities, suburbs, and infrastructure. We harvest an increasing amount of non-renewable natural resources. We convert wilderness into agricultural land, and produce an unlimited supply of consumer goods.

All of these activities result in pollution – from pesticides, greenhouse gases, industrial waste, and enough garbage to cover the planet's entire surface – and the destruction of wildlife habitat. Indeed so spectacular has been the march of human 'progress' that every single living system on the planet is in rapid decline.[2] Humans have inadvertently killed billions, maybe even trillions of animals and exterminated entire species. As *New Internationalist* editor Richard Swift observes: 'We are pushing a hundred species a day, four species an hour, into evolutionary oblivion.'[3]

## Hidden cruelty

According to the Animal Alliance of Canada, human 'progress' is 'the hidden cruelty'.[4] It is estimated that by the end of the 21st century, two-thirds of all the animals on the planet today will be extinct.[5] Yet even animal activists often fail to see the connection between the growth of our civilization and animal suffering. Many don't consider how the consumption of fossil fuels, agricultural products and consumer goods impact animals' lives. While PETA founder Ingrid Newkirk has recently written a book called *Making Kind Choices* that explores some of these connections, most AR organizations focus on overt cruelty to animals in the quest for 'progress', as opposed to the equally devastating 'hidden cruelty'.

Scientific and technological advancement, as well as the development and manufacture of consumer products, claims the lives of over 100 million animals every year.[6] Animal experimentation, or vivisection, is perhaps the most controversial issue. The scientific community insists that animal experiments have greatly benefited humans, by allowing us to produce products and medicines that have greatly improved our quality of life and health. Animal activists, on the other hand, argue that animal experimentation is unethical because it causes intense physical and emotional suffering to millions of animals every year. While the public seems to think that it is wrong to impose pain on animals for the development of non-essential goods (such as cosmetics testing), the testing of 'trivial' items is still routine. Animal activists have been quick to point out that cosmetics, cleaning products, industrial chemicals, food additives and manufactured goods are customarily tested on animals. Almost two-thirds of animal experiments conducted have little or nothing to do with human health and medicine.[7]

A much less clear-cut issue is the validity of animal experiments for medical research. Public opinion generally supports animal experiments in this field because it considers the development of medical technology to be essential to human health. However, animal activists suggest that this is in fact a myth and that real gains in human wellbeing haven't been due to new medicinal technology but rather improved nutrition and sanitation.[8] And while some activists merely oppose animal experimentation for non-essential products and technologies, others believe that it is inherently immoral to inflict pain on an animal even if it will significantly improve or even save human lives.

### The Draize Test

The testing of products on animals became widespread in the 1950s, largely as a result of the growth of the pharmaceutical and petrochemical industries. Companies wanted to market the chemicals they had created and animal testing seemed to be the best and cheapest way to test a product's safety for human use. Currently many countries require that new chemical compounds are tested on animals before going on the market to ensure that they are not carcinogenic or otherwise harmful to humans – although this is not foolproof, as seen in a recent UK case where six men suffered organ failure hours after taking the rheumatoid arthritis drug TGN1412 during a trial; the drug had been tested on rabbits and monkeys.

The Draize Test is the most well-known irritancy test. Developed in 1944, it 'involves dripping the test substance into a rabbit's eye and recording the damage over three to twenty-one days. Scientists use rabbits for these tests because rabbits' eyes have no tear ducts to wash away the irritant, and their eyes are large enough for any inflammation to be clearly visible.' Animals subjected to the Draize Test have to be restrained to prevent them from clawing at their eyes.[4] Depending on the substance, the eye may only be slightly irritated; it may be ulcerated; or it may be burned out of the socket completely.[9]

## Some of the experiments that have been done on animals

- Rats kept awake for 33 days to see how they would behave with sleep deprivation – they suffered severe pathology and death (University of Chicago).
- Mice had forelimbs amputated at birth to see if they would continue grooming (University of Oregon).
- Male rats starved to see if it affected their sexual behavior (Oxford University).
- 10-day-old kittens have their eyes sewn shut to monitor the effects of sight deprivation (Oxford University).
- Herpes virus injected into the brains of mice (Cambridge University).
- Nerve gases, cyanide, radiation, guns and missiles used on monkeys (standard government defense research).
- Pigs and monkeys used as 'crash-test dummies' (General Motors).
- Baby monkeys separated from mothers at birth and given a mechanical replacement that violently shook them to gauge effects of maternal deprivation and fear (Primate Research Center, Wisconsin).
- Pig fetuses decapitated while still in mothers' wombs to see how it affected the sows' body chemistry (US Department of Agriculture).
- Beagles injected with plutonium (Harvard University).
- Monkeys' fingers amputated to see how the brain perceives parts of the body (University of California, San Francisco). ■

Source: Robert Sharpe, *The Cruel Deception* (Thorsons, 1988).

## Animals and 'progress'

The Lethal Dose Fifty Per Cent test (or LD50) is used to determine toxicity. 'The test is used to determine the dosage of a given substance that is required to kill 50 per cent of the test animals within a specified time period.'[4] The animals are repeatedly force-fed, injected, or forced to inhale the test substance, sometimes for up to a period of four years.[10] The practice of force-feeding large amounts of even relatively harmless substances can be very damaging – many animals suffer from blockages and ruptures because of it. Researchers often use mice and rats for this kind of toxicity test because they are unable to vomit.[11] Continual exposure to more toxic substances also causes extensive internal damage and many animals suffer from chronic diarrhea, convulsions and massive hemorrhaging before they die.[4]

## Diseases

Medical research makes much use of animals in the development of new medications, in the study of human diseases, and in psychological and behavioral studies. New treatments are developed by observing their reaction in animal subjects and are then tested extensively on them to make sure they won't cause damage to human patients. For disease research, infections such as HIV are injected into animals so researchers can observe how they affect specific parts of animals' bodies. For diseases that can't simply be injected into the animal, such as cancer, diabetes, arthritis and cardiovascular disease, animals are exposed to carcinogens or have their bodies manipulated to replicate the symptoms.

In both cases animals are observed, dissected and given experimental treatment to relieve the infections or diseases. Psychological and behavioral studies make use of a disproportionate number of non-human primates because they are similar to humans. Common tests involve maternal deprivation, starvation, water deprivation, electric shock, forced immobilization, drug addiction, and brain damage.[12] The details of all these kinds of medical studies have been well documented (see classics such as Richard Ryder's *Victims of Science*, and Peter Singer's *Animal Liberation*). Needless to say, animals used in medical studies suffer tremendously, and the majority without the benefits of anesthetic. According to the British Union for the Abolition of Vivisection (BUAV) in 2004, 61 per cent of animals used in tests were not given anesthetic.[13]

Most animals used in scientific experiments are bred in factory-farm like conditions to supply laboratories. They are 'born to die'.[13] In addition, most of them never live outside the lab setting. This means they are confined for their entire lives to barren cages with little exercise, stimulation or social interaction. For example, in one Canadian lab, rats are given one piece of paper towel a week to shred, for 'enrichment'.[14] Because many lab animals are used in long-term and repeated studies, their confinement alone can lead to serious physical and psychological distress.

**Medical research**
One of the major problems with medical research is that it justifies the use of animals for studies that have no direct relationship with human health. The pursuit of 'general' scientific knowledge leads some researchers to burn, break the limbs, crush the organs, electrically shock, and sew shut the eyes of lab animals, for example. Scientists have been doing these kinds of experiments for hundreds of years to satisfy their general curiosity about animal physiology. In Canada in 1996, of all animals reported to have been used in experiments that caused severe pain, only about 14 per cent were used for general scientific research and less than 4 per cent were used in studies directly relating to human or animal health. The rest were to get products approved for sale.[15]

## Animals and 'progress'

Another problem that AR activists have with animal research is that it is often very badly regulated. Some countries, such as Britain and Australia, require researchers to apply for licenses and justify their use of animal experiments to an ethics committee. They also have rules about the use of anesthesia for painful experiments.

However, these kinds of regulations do not exist in many countries, including Canada and the US. In Canada there is no federal law that regulates animal research, only a set of industry guidelines monitored by the Canadian Council on Animal Care, that apply to institutions that have been given federal money. Private labs owned by corporations are not required to follow these guidelines.[14] In the US, where the majority of the world's animal research is conducted, the Animal Welfare Act regulates the transportation, handling and housing of animals, but not actual research practices. In other words, a researcher can, theoretically, be charged with housing animals in unsanitary conditions but not for beating or mutilating it without anesthetic. In addition, the American Animal Welfare Act doesn't apply to rodents (or birds, fish, and reptiles) which comprise the majority of lab animals used.

Partly due to poor regulation, there is a good deal of repetition in animal research. Because most researchers do not have to justify their animal use, many conduct experiments that have already been done in the past. Even a simple regulation that required scientists to research the existing literature for the test results they are looking for would significantly reduce animal suffering. Because so much animal research is either repetitive or trivial, it has been estimated that 75 per cent of such work never makes it into print in medical journals.[8] In addition, of all the medications developed, about 80 per cent are so-called 'me-too' drugs which are 'minor molecular modifications of older and well-established products'. These new medicines, which governments require to be tested on animals, have much more commercial than therapeutic value because pharmaceutical companies can get patent rights to them. Pharmaceutical companies develop them to increase their profit margin, but many animals suffer needlessly.[12]

## Diseases of affluence

A more serious problem is that the drug companies don't actually develop the medications that are crucial for the majority of the world's illnesses. Only 1 per cent of research money goes into research for developing treatment for diseases that are rampant in the Majority World (with the exception of HIV/AIDS). Most of the cash goes into finding treatment for the 'diseases of affluence' in the West, such as diabetes, high blood pressure, heart disease, strokes, obesity and anxiety.[12] Currently 80 per cent of the drugs manufactured are directed at people living in developed countries, which comprise only 20 per cent of the world's population.[16] While many Western diseases are caused by lifestyle and environment, very little research money goes into prevention efforts.[17]

This is because profits are made from treatment, but not from preventing or curing diseases.

In fact, treatment already exists for the diseases that kill the majority of people on the planet, such as malaria and tuberculosis. If we applied our current medical knowledge to the world, most premature death could be eradicated.[8] TB, for example, kills one person every 15 seconds, and has been treatable for 60 years.[18] However, because it is common only in the developing world, manufacturing treatment isn't a lucrative business for pharmaceutical companies. As Joel Bakan, co-author of *The Corporation*, puts it, the pharmaceutical companies make 'more money from drugs to treat baldness and impotence than they would from drugs to treat diseases... that are the leading causes of death in the developing world.'[16] So, animals are experimented upon to develop drugs, many of which are non-essential, for a tiny proportion of the world's population – while existing drugs that don't require any further testing are not developed because they won't bring in profits, even though they could save millions of lives.

Some animal experiments may be unavoidable, but a good many could easily be substituted by other research methods. Significant progress has been made in the development of in vitro tests – which use human tissues and cultures and micro-organisms to determine toxicity. Careful clinical and epidemiological studies, as well as the use of new imaging technology, could also be used instead of repeating tests on animals.

## Misleading

Research shows that these tests are in fact more accurate than animal-based ones. For example, in vitro tests are at least 11 per cent more accurate than animal tests in determining toxicity[19] and the US Congress Office of Technological Assessment has declared that epidemiological studies are more useful than animal studies in pinning down the causes of most human illnesses.[17] This is because human and animal physiology, chemistry, cellular and molecular make-up, circulation, and digestion are vastly different. Scientists are still unable to replicate most human diseases in animals, even in primates who share 97-99 per cent of our DNA, and more than 50 per cent of drugs that have passed animal trials are later found unfit for human consumption[17] (see p 74).

Despite this, and the fact that many scientists consider animal tests to be misleading, millions of animals are still used in labs every year. Many companies have made efforts to reduce their dependence on animal testing. Partially as a result of public campaigns, by the late 1980s many of the big-name cosmetic companies (such as Mary Kay, Revlon, Avon and Fabergé) had agreed to stop animal testing. Gillette, which manufactures shaving and oral care products, antiperspirants, batteries and Braun appliances, have not used animal tests in over 10 years. However, despite the gains made in the late 1980s and early 1990s, the numbers of animals used in experiments began to increase again in the mid-1990s, largely because of developments in the biotechnology industry. In 1998, for the first year since 1976, the number of animals used in research increased. Numbers have been slowly creeping up ever since.[13] As writer Charlotte Montgomery has revealed, this is largely due to the increase in the use of 'transgenic' animals being created in labs for the purpose of manufacturing organs that can be harvested for human use. Pharmaceutical companies around the world are investing billions of dollars to develop this technol-

## Premarin

While some animals are being genetically altered so that they will produce pharmaceuticals, some don't need to be. Pregnant horses are currently being 'pharmed' for their urine, which is rich in estrogen. Marketed under the name Premarin by Wyeth-Ayerst Laboratories, this estrogen is used to treat menopausal symptoms. Premarin is the most commonly prescribed drug in the US. While estrogen can be synthetically produced, Wyeth-Ayerst prefers to harvest it from mares. More than 75,000 mares are kept permanently pregnant in the US and Canada. Their foals are the byproduct of the industry – more than 70,000 are killed every year. The mares used to produce Premarin are exploited to the fullest. They are immediately separated from their foals and impregnated again only days after birth. They are kept in such cramped conditions that they can't lie down properly and many become lame as a result. They have only limited access to water so that their urine will be more concentrated – this often leads to renal and liver problems. Finally, once mares are too old to give birth successfully, they are slaughtered and used in pet food. Premarin is the only estrogen replacement therapy that is animal-derived. ■

Source: American Anti-Vivisection Society, www.aavs.org

ogy.[14] While so far all attempts at animal-human transplants have failed, it is estimated that by 2010 in the US alone the 'xenotransplantation' market will exceed $6 billion a year.[17] Primates and pigs are the animals of choice in transgenic research; by 1996 the use of primates, which declined in the early 1990s, had reached pre-1989 levels.[14]

## Cloned animals

Dr Richard Nicholson, editor of *The Bulletin of Medical Ethics*, calculates that if xenotransplantation is successfully developed, it will only increase life expectancy by about 0.02 per cent – a matter of weeks.[20] However the biotech industry is busily developing cloned animals that contain human genes because it is estimated that the organs will sell for $10,000-18,000, and will increase the use of expensive transplant drugs.[14] Other scientists are working on manipulating animals so that their milk or blood will contain valuable pharmaceuticals. If successful, these animals will be 'pharmed' to produce treatments for humans. Researchers have started working on producing a blood clotting agent (AAT) in sheep. The market for this drug alone is estimated to be worth about $100 million.[20]

Not all genetically modified animals are being created for medical purposes. Work has been done to engineer pigs' immune systems so that they will attack fat cells to create leaner meat, or grow at astonishing rates to produce more meat. Researchers are also working to create a sheep that will shed its own wool without shearing, and poultry that is born without feathers.[14,20] Nexia Biotechnologies has inserted a spider gene into a goat so that its milk will contain spider silk, which may be used in bulletproof vests.[21] One company is currently taking orders on a hypoallergenic cat that it hasn't yet successfully created, but plans to have on the market by 2007.[22] These kinds of experiments cause huge suffering in the trial animals – deformity, tumors, abnormal organ development and premature death are common in genetically altered animals, though not often reported in the media.[14] For example, producing one successfully cloned animal requires killing approximately 98 other animals in the process.[6] Animal activists are also concerned that animals used in transgenic research face particularly miserable conditions since, in order to prevent contamination, they need to be kept totally isolated from other animals in completely sterile environments. Because many of the animals used in transgenic research, such as primates and pigs, are intelligent and bore easily, they live lives of 'inevitable loneliness and deprivation'.[14]

The creation of transgenic animals also poses broader ethical problems because it has opened the door for the patenting of animals. When pharmaceutical companies alter even one of an animal's genes, they can claim ownership of that animal and all of its offspring (or cloned replicas). This has already happened with plants and has sparked a huge international controversy because farmers are being forced to pay for the seeds they have produced from patented plants.

### Blueprints of life

However, the patenting of animal genes may have even more far-reaching consequences because it turns living beings into human inventions, or commodities, which can be privately owned. Animal patenting allows corporations to own, and profit from, all 'blueprints of life' on the planet. Imagine if one company held the rights to all tiger DNA and could alter it and sell it for its own purposes? The patenting of animals reinforces the view that something is only valuable if it is owned privately and has a market value.[2]

As it stands, patents on mammals already exist and pharmaceutical companies are frantically scouring the world for any genes that might have a market. In 1988, the US Patent and Trademark Office granted the first patent on a mammal – a lab mouse predisposed to cancer, known as the 'oncomouse'. In 1993, the European Patent Office agreed to grant the patent as well.[23] So far, 470 patents exist for animals, such as mice, cats, dogs, sheep, pigs, cattle and primates. Thousands more are pending. Before the 1980s it was illegal to patent any living organism; now the only restriction on patenting is the genes of naturally born humans.

---

## Traditional cures and animals

Humans have been using animals and animal parts to cure illnesses for thousands of years. Traditional Chinese medicine, for example, uses extracts from animal bones and organs to cure a variety of illnesses. However, this has led to serious conservation problems in Asia. Loss of wildlife habitat and growing demands for Chinese medicine around the world had led to a drastic decline in some animal populations. Some of the most popular treatments are derived from seriously endangered animals – such as tigers, bears, rhinos and sea turtles. Conservation groups are working with traditional practitioners and Asian governments to promote alternative treatments so that threatened species can recover.[1]

Many non-endangered species are also used in traditional medicine. However their use poses welfare concerns, particularly when they are farmed. Elk are raised around the world for their antler velvet, which is used in tonics to treat a variety of disorders from anemia to low sperm count. Elk antlers are made out of live tissue and must be cut off the live animal. Mature elks can produce up to 30 pounds of velvet a year as their antlers grow back. The velvet sells for up to $500/pound.[2] Bears are also farmed. In an effort to protect endangered bears in the wild that were being hunted for their gallbladders, producers turned to farming in the 1980s. Factory farmed bears live for up to 20 years in tiny cages, from which they are 'milked' of their gall bile every day.[3] Because 'harvesting' these products is extremely painful and in most cases plant-based alternatives exist, animal advocates are asking practitioners to stop prescribing animal products to their patients. ■

Sources: 1 World Wildlife Fund/World Wildlife Fund for Nature, www.wwf.org
2 Charlotte Montgomery, *Blood Relations* (Between the Lines, 2000).
3 Animals Asia, 'China Bear Rescue', (pamphlet).

Animal activists believe that the way scientific research is conducted today is unethical. They believe that at the very least, all unnecessary experiments (those that are either repetitive, can be done using other models, or for non-essential products) should be banned. They point out that the research industry is driven more by profit than humanitarian concerns and that animals shouldn't be forced to suffer for this.[10] While many AR organizations are working toward achieving specific reforms, most believe that animal testing is inherently wrong, even when it contributes to technology that can save human lives. Abolitionist organizations, such as the American Anti-Vivisection Society, BUAV and the Japan Anti-Vivisection Association, argue that only non-animal methods should ever be used in scientific and medical research. They believe that because animals are capable of suffering they should never be subjected to experimentation.

## Recent victories

While most activists prefer to use constitutional methods to abolish animal experiments (protests, education campaigns, petitioning), others are willing to break the law to save animals from science. Animal activists, many of whom identify as ALF members, have conducted several hundred raids on labs and lab-breeding facilities around the world since the early 1980s. They have taken photographs of gruesome secret experiments, destroyed millions of dollars' worth of equipment, and in some cases, actually set the animals free. Lab raids have slowed down in recent years, largely because of increased security at research facilities.

However the campaign against animal testing is alive and well, particularly in Britain, where animal rights issues have wide popular support. In the last ten years, the Stop Huntingdon Animal Cruelty (SHAC) campaign has managed to close down several breeding and research facilities. In 1997, the group that became SHAC pressured Consort Kennels to close down and rescued 200 beagle puppies bred for experimentation. It then turned its attention to Hillgrove Cat Farm, and by 1999 the facility closed and 800 cats were rescued. Since then, SHAC has targeted the research company, Huntingdon Life Sciences. The organization has put pressure on the company's clients, suppliers and insurance providers, and has brought forward lawsuits against HLS, in an attempt to put it out of business.

### Protests

The SHAC campaign led to such a massive decrease in HLS's contracts and increases in its expenditures that in 2001 the company closed up shop and moved its operations to the US. SHAC is confident that HLS is 'financially dead in the water' and will eventually have to close all its facilities.[24] Other groups in Britain have also seen successes. In 2003, plans to construct a primate lab at Cambridge University were abandoned after massive protests organized by SPEAC (Stop Primate Experiments at Cambridge).

Since then plans have gone ahead to build a similar lab at Oxford University. Feeling betrayed that public opinion has been disregarded, SPEAC (now SPEAK) and other anti-vivisection groups have launched a campaign against the new facility, which would be the largest primate lab in Europe. In 2004, Montpellier, the major contractor for the Oxford lab, pulled out of its $18 million contract because of pressure from the anti-vivisection community and construction was halted for 16 months. While construction started again in December 2005 and the names of the companies involved have remained secret, SPEAK plans to continue its campaign until Oxford University agrees to cancel the project.[25]

Years of lobbying have also helped convince governments that alternatives need to be found for animal testing. Most Western governments have invested money in the development of alternative testing models. In addition, the European Commission has tried to create uniform laws regarding animal experiments so that tests will not be duplicated in different countries and alternatives models will be explored before an experiment on animals is done. So far, Britain, Germany and the Netherlands have implemented the Commission's guidelines and France and Italy are considering them.[26] Germany, the Netherlands and Slovakia have already implemented bans on cosmetics testing, and Britain has banned the use of testing for cosmetics, alcohol and tobacco research. Anglo-US Asterand is a cutting-edge pharmaceutical company that has banned all animal testing and relies solely on *in vitro* testing.[5] Britain and New Zealand/Aotearoa have also implemented a testing ban on the Great Apes (chimpanzees, gorillas, orangutans, bonobos), which is a huge step toward breaking down the human/primate divide.[27] Norway only develops drugs that are needed so that animal tests aren't done for drugs that replicate ones already on the market, and Switzerland is at the head of the pack, making efforts to phase out animal testing altogether.[12, 27]

**Minimizing pain**

Progress has also been made in India. Much of the pharmaceutical industry there is owned by members of the Jain community, some of whom (although certainly not all) make efforts to minimize the amount of pain caused by tests and run facilities to rehabilitate and release lab animals after the tests are finished.[28] The Indian Government has also prohibited the export of live monkeys to be used in laboratories in the West, and has made dissection optional for students.[29]

While North America is lagging on laboratory reforms, some American states have banned the painful Draize test and the dissection of animals in schools. Currently two-thirds of all American medical schools no longer rely on animal dissection. Canada has prohibited the patenting of animal genes, which is very good news for lab animals.

These kinds of successes give the animal rights movement optimism that the campaign against animal experiments is actually influencing decision-makers. While many animals continue to suffer in labs, their numbers have, overall, decreased since the 1970s in large part because of the efforts of activists. Many organizations are dedicated to continuing their struggle until animal testing has been abolished completely.

**1** Ronald Wright, *A Short History of Progress* (Anansi Press, 2004). **2** Mark Achbar and Joel Bakan, *The Corporation* (documentary), (Zeitgeist Films, 2004). **3** Richard Swift, 'Endangered Species: Who's Next?' *New Internationalist* No 288, March 1997. **4** Animal Alliance of Canada, www.animalalliance.ca **5** Matthew Scully, *Dominion* (St Martin's Press, 2002). **6** People for the Ethical Treatment of Animals, www.peta.org **7** Canadian Council on Animal Care, 2001 Report, quoted by People for the Ethical Treatment of Animals, www.peta.org **8** Peter Singer, *Animal Liberation* 3rd edition (Pimlico, 1995). **9** Tom Regan, *All That Dwell Therein* (University of California Press, 1982). **10** Robert Garner, *Animals, Politics and Morality* (Manchester University Press, 1993). **11** Tom Regan, *Empty Cages* (Rowman and Littlefield, 2004). **12** Robert Sharpe, *The Cruel Deception* (Thorsons Publishing, 1988). **13** British Union for the Abolition of Vivisection, www.buav.org **14** Charlotte Montgomery, *Blood Relations* (Between the Lines, 2000). **15** Based on statistics from Charlotte Montgomery, *Blood Relations* (Between the Lines, 2000). **16** Joel Bakan, *The Corporation* (Viking, 2004). **17** CR Greek, MD and JS Greek DVM, *Sacred Cows and Golden Geese* (Continuum, 2000). **18** Médecins Sans Frontières, *Dispatches*, volume 7. **19** American Anti-Vivisection Society, www.aavs.org **20** Danny Penman, 'Flying Pigs and Featherless Chickens', *New Internationalist* 293, August 1997. **21** *The New York Times*, 1 May 2000. **22** CNN News, www.cnn.com/2004/TECH/10/27/biotechnology.cats/ **23** 'Genes – The Facts', *New Internationalist* No 293, August 1997. **24** SHAC Newsletter, May 2004. **25** *The Guardian*, 21 July 2004 and 3 March 2006. **26** Lewis Petrinovich, *Darwinian Dominion* (MIT Press, 1999). **27** Richard Ryder, *The Political Animal* (McFarland, 1998). **28** Christopher Chapple, *Nonviolence to Animals, Earth and Self in Asian Traditions* (State University of New York Press, 1993). **29** Beauty Without Cruelty India, www.bwcindia.org

# 6 Animals and fashion

*'The animals of the world exist for their own reasons. They were not made for humans any more than black people were made for white, or women created for men.'*

– ALICE WALKER (1944 -   ), AUTHOR

**The fur, leather and wool trades perpetuate the mistreatment of animals as well as many of the workers in the industry.**

HUMANS HAVE ALWAYS used animal products for clothing. The first nomadic peoples used skins and furs from animals they hunted and later, farming societies also used wool and leather from domesticated animals. However the ways in which early humans procured materials to clothe themselves changed dramatically with industrialization and later globalization. While fur, wool and leather were once mostly obtained locally and only in sufficient quantities to provide for basic needs, the dictates of fashion are now felt across all sectors of society. Since the mass production of clothes and shoes began in the late 19th century, people in industrialized countries have been encouraged to buy more and have been better able to afford to follow fashion trends. Today, the clothing and shoe industries are international in scope and are geared more towards making a profit than providing necessities.

Fur was once an essential commodity. People living in northern climates relied on animal skins to stay warm and dry during the winter. As the human population increased, fur-bearing animals became scarce in Europe, because of excessive hunting and land clearing for agriculture. Wolves and bears, for example, were extinct in Britain by the 17th century. As fur-bearing animals became scarce, fur

increasingly became associated with the upper eche-
lons of society. The lower classes used cheaper alternatives, such as wool and other textiles. Ever since, fur
has been a fashion item in most places in the world.
Today, fur is still a symbol of wealth and status in
many cultures. However, during the 20th century,
more and more people, particularly in the West, could
afford fur and so the industry expanded. Fur farming
was established to create a steady supply of pelts to
make up for dwindling wild stock.

### Fashion *faux pas*

Activists have been targeting the fur industry for
years, largely because fur has become a luxury item
in industrialized societies. The modern campaign
started in the late 1950s with the founding of Lady
Muriel Dowding's Beauty Without Cruelty campaign
in Britain and culminated in the 1987 fur market
crash. Along with the anti-cosmetic-testing campaign,
the anti-fur campaign remains the largest and most
successful the animal rights movement has ever
launched. Celebrities jumped on board, refused to
wear fur at fashion shows and posed for PETA ads. By
the 1990s, wearing fur was considered a fashion *faux
pas* in many circles and the market plummeted.

However in the last few years, fur has made a
dramatic comeback. In the late 1990s, the industry
tried to prop up its dwindling market by supplying
fur to designers free of charge to encourage them to
start using it again.[1] The strategy worked; at first
designers used brightly dyed furs so they wouldn't
appear too real, but now fur *au naturel* is popular
again. Even full-length coats have reappeared. Ten
years ago, most people didn't dare to wear these coats
in public, but now they are back in style, and are once
again a common sight in wealthy neighborhoods and
at fashion shows. Celebrities who eschewed fur in the
1990s – such as Cindy Crawford who posed wearing

an anti-fur button for PETA – are now donning animal skins. While fur is still found mostly on the backs of the rich, the fur industry is trying to 'democratize' by developing marketing strategies to appeal to 'a larger group of consumers at a wide range of price points'.[2] The marketing of the fur-trimmed parka is a part of this strategy – now many more people can afford the privilege of wearing fur.

## Fur trapping

While public opinion may have changed since the 1990s, the methods for producing fur have not. Animal advocates stress that fur production, whether from farmed or wild animals, is excessively cruel. There are several methods for trapping animals. The leghold trap is made of a toothed metal clamp that closes around the animal's leg or foot. This kind of trap is considered particularly cruel because about a quarter of animals manage to escape by chewing their foot off.[3] Most of these animals die slowly from blood loss, infection or the inability to procure food. Animals also can knock their teeth out from trying to chew through the trap. Because trappers have many traps to check it takes an average of 15 hours to retrieve and kill a trapped animal. These hours are filled with tremendous suffering for the animal.[4] However in areas that are more geographically remote, such as parts of Russia and Canada, it can take a week to retrieve an animal which has usually died from starvation, hypothermia, or predation. If an animal is still alive when the trapper finds it, it needs to be killed in a way that will not damage the pelt – clubbing and kicking are common methods.[3]

Semi-aquatic animals, like beavers, are trapped in the water. After a limb is caught eventually the weight of the trap pulls the animal underwater and it drowns. This is clearly a quicker and more humane way to kill an animal but it is not anywhere near painless, as semi-aquatic animals can survive underwater for about 20 minutes (and sometimes longer). Another method is the 'conibear' trap, which is designed to instantly kill an animal by breaking its back. The problem is that if a beast either larger or smaller than the target animal is caught, the mechanism doesn't work properly and can cause severe injury without death. Even these 'humane' alternatives cause great distress.

Trapping is indiscriminate. It is estimated that as many as 2 out of every 3 animals trapped are non-target species. In the US alone, 4-6 million of these 'trash' animals are caught every year. 'Trash' can include anything from pets to endangered species. There have been many reports of dogs and bald eagles being caught in the US.[3,4]

Apart from threatening endangered species, trapping can also have other serious consequences for local ecosystems. Because most animals trapped for fur are predators, excessive trapping can lead to an overabundance of prey species, many of which are forced to encroach on human environments to find enough food to survive. Trapping also often kills healthy animals as opposed to sick or weak animals that would naturally die; in this sense, when conducted on a large scale, it undermines population stability and the long-term viability of a species.[3]

### Trapping and aboriginal rights

In North America about one per cent of the animals killed for fur are caught by aboriginal hunters who depend on hunting for their livelihood.[5] Because this number is so small, many AR activists sidestep the issue of aboriginal hunting and prefer to focus on the international fur industry. This is problematic, however, because many subsistence hunters sell the pelts of the animals they hunt to the companies that manufacture fur garments worldwide. Therefore, the collapse of the fur industry also means a decline in their standard of living and their ability to buy the consumer goods they need to survive. Some animal activists have suggested that aboriginal peoples should therefore abandon their hunting practices and become assimilated into the majority culture.[6]

The seal hunt, in particular, has provoked international controversy. The scale of commercial hunting and the methods used to kill seals have spurred international outrage. In response to the campaign against seal hunting in the 1980s, the US and the EU banned the import of whitecoats (the pelts from seal pups). Many people around the world have also boycotted adult seal pelts. This has resulted in a serious loss of income for Inuit communities in Canada, Alaska and Greenland, who have hunted seals for hundreds of years.

Contemporary Inuit hunters use snowmobiles and rifles to hunt seals. Because of their use of modern technology, some AR groups involved in the anti-sealing campaign argue that they have renounced their right to engage in hunting because they have given up traditional methods. However, seal meat continues to be one of the staples of the Inuit diet and this is their primary reason for hunting them. They sell their seal pelts so that they can buy snowmobiles, gasoline, ammunition and dry food goods, which are today essential commodities in the Arctic.[6]

Inuit hunters were never responsible for the extermination of seal populations or for the cruelties of the whitecoat hunt; they hunt 99 per cent adult seals. However, their lifestyle is being threatened by the boycott on the sealing industry because they rely on income from seal pelts. This is a difficult issue that AR activists must confront when condemning the seal (and whale) industries in particular, and the larger fur industry in general. By opposing hunting, activists run the risk of alienating people who are potential allies in the struggle against industrial animal exploitation, and perpetuating 'a continuing colonial process in the North'.[6] AR activists, many of whom are also sensitive to the rights of native people, are likely aware of this tension and this may be why they generally remain silent on the issue of aboriginal hunting.

## Fur farms

Farming produces over 75 per cent of the world's fur – every year almost 30 million animals are slaughtered on fur farms.[7] The business was established in the early 20th century, when animals in the wild became scarce in areas where they had previously been abundant. Like most farming nowadays, fur farming is conducted intensively. The animals are kept in small wire mesh cages (similar to battery cages for chickens) in large warehouses until they are large enough to be slaughtered. Mink is the most farmed fur-bearing animal, followed by fox.[7] It is estimated that there are currently more mink on fur farms than in the wild.

In addition, the HSUS estimates that about two million cat and dog pelts end up on the North American market every year, exported from Asian countries that raise them intensively for meat and

**Fashion victims**
An average full-length fur coat requires one of the following:

**8** seals
**16** coyotes
**18** lynx
**20** otters
**40** raccoons
**42** foxes
**50** sables or muskrats
**60** minks

Source: Tom Regan, *Empty Cages* (Rowman and Littlefield, 2004).

market their fur as rabbit or 'Asian wolf'.[4] Conditions on fur farms are notoriously bad. The animals do not 'need' to be kept healthy because only their fur will be used. Therefore infections, diseases and injuries are usually left untreated. Parasites, such as ticks, lice, mites and fleas are also common. Fur-bearing animals have only been bred for a few generations and fur farms often supplement their stock with animals from the wild. Because of this, the animals show signs of severe psychosis, like their counterparts in zoos and circuses.

Mink for example have a natural range of up to 2,500 acres, but on farms they are kept in cages the size of two shoeboxes, which don't give them enough room to stand upright. Despite being semi-aquatic animals who spend up to 60 per cent of their time in water, they are denied access to water except for drinking. These conditions cause incredible suffering. About 30 per cent of farmed mink engage in self-mutilation. Cannibalism is also common.

Predators, such as foxes, have an even wider range than mink but are kept in groups of four in cages only 2.5 square meters. Because of their intensive confinement, they too engage in self-mutilation, cannibalism and other psychotic behavior.[3,7] Farmed animals are killed by poisoning, genital and anal electrocution, suffocation and neck-breaking. Humane slaughter laws do not apply to fur-bearing animals, so they can legally be slaughtered while conscious.

Many AR advocates consider fur farming even more cruel than trapping because animals live their entire lives in misery before dying. Because farmed animals are mostly wild, their confinement causes even more suffering than it does for domesticated livestock. For this reason, fur farms have been particularly targeted by the AR movement.

According to one estimate, between 1995 and 1999, tens of thousands of fur farm animals were set free by animal activists in some 60 raids.[8]

## Animals and fashion

Although AR activists find it upsetting that fur is once again a fashion item, the fur industry has not come anywhere near recovering from its collapse in the late 1980s. At present, just below 40 million animals are killed every year for fur, while in 1990 about 70 million were killed annually.[9] Many people still avoid fur and choose to wear clever imitations. Nonetheless, PETA has re-launched its anti-fur campaign and has recruited many celebrities who 'would rather go naked than wear fur'. In a controversial move, the campaign group has started distributing old donated fur coats

### Foot fetish

Increasing consumer demand for goods that rely on animal products such as leather shoes, serves to prop up the whole animal industry.

| Annual consumption of footwear per capita | |
| --- | --- |
| Country | Number of Pairs |
| United States | 6.2 |
| Denmark | 5.8 |
| France | 5.6 |
| Britain | 5.1 |
| Vietnam | 0.4 |

Source: 'The Leather Global Value Chain and the World Leather Footwear Market', www.factbook.net/leather_evolution.php

to homeless shelters in New York City in an attempt to reduce the prestige associated with fur. The organization hopes to remind the fashion industry why it rejected fur 15 years ago.

### Leather

The most commonly worn animal skins come from domesticated animals – mostly cows and pigs. Valued for its durability, leather is one of the most widely used textiles in the world. If you walk down the street or ride on a bus, you'll notice that almost everyone is wearing leather shoes or belts. This came about in part because, after fur went out of style, many designers started replacing it with leather. Leather coats, pants, skirts and tops became popular. In the

US, leather sales went up from $900 million a year in 1991 to $2.7 billion a year by 1999.[10] The international trade in cow leather quadrupled between 1979 and 1996.[11] However leather products don't only come from cows and pigs but also from kangaroos, alligators and snakes (the last two are farmed for their skins).

Many people, even those who avoid eating animal products, believe that leather is simply a byproduct of the meat industry and that wearing it is not directly supporting the killing of animals. However AR activists argue that the two are inextricably linked. They stress that leather is actually a 'co-product' of the meat industry and that the market value of domesticated animals takes into account the price of their skins.[12] They suggest that to effectively boycott the factory farm system, individuals must give up leather as well as animal food products. The facts speak for themselves – leather as a commodity is worth slightly more on the world market than meat.[11]

The leather industry is truly global. While both North America and Europe produce many animals whose hides could be used for leather, they import most of their leather goods from Asia. Asia is currently the largest exporter, and supplies 78 per cent of the world's leather.[11] So despite the fact that several million cows and pigs are slaughtered every year in North America, their skins aren't used for leather.

Animal welfare activists have been particularly concerned about the leather industry in China and India (two large world suppliers). They point out that since animal welfare and humane slaughter laws are much less strict in China than in the West, consumers should avoid Chinese leather.

However, in India the situation is even worse because the majority of cattle slaughter is done on an illegal black market, and therefore is not regulated at all. Because it is illegal to kill cows in many parts of India, the infrastructure does not exist for the proper transport and slaughter of cows, and cows killed are routinely subjected to gross mistreatment. While many animal rights groups oppose the leather industry in general, they have asked retailers to boycott leather from India in particular.

## Wool

Wool seems like the most benign animal product we wear – we simply shear away excess hair without having to kill the animal. But many AR activists, who criticize fur and leather use, also avoid wool products. They argue that regardless of the fact that shearing wool doesn't directly kill sheep, the process disregards the animals' best interests.

Unlike other domesticated farm animals, most of the world's sheep do not live in factory farms. Most sheep, except for the ones that produce luxury wool, live outside. Free-roaming sheep are a common sight in many parts of Britain, South Africa, Australia and New Zealand. The sheep are largely left to themselves until they are herded for shearing. While this is obviously much better for the animals than being raised intensively on a factory farm, many sheep die from exposure or neglect every year. It is estimated that in Australia, the world's largest wool exporter, 20-40 per cent of lambs, and 8 million mature sheep, die every year.[13]

Shearing itself is a frightening and painful experience for sheep because it is done in an assembly-line fashion. The beasts are clamped by the head and quickly shaved to the skin from top to bottom. Most get their skin cut during the process. Serious wounds occur when teats and genitals get caught in the blade. Shearing also is a serious shock to the sheep's system. Because they are not equipped to tolerate the elements without their fleece, many die from exposure in the winter and suffer from sunburn in the summer.[4]

AR activists in Australia are particularly opposed to the production of merino wool. Merino sheep have been bred to have folds of skin so that they will produce more wool. However because they are not native to Australia, they have not adapted well to the summer heat. In warm weather, blowflies lay their eggs in between the folds in the skin, particularly around the genitals where feces has collected. When the eggs hatch, the maggots feed on the sheep and can eventually kill it. There are several ways to deal with this problem – such as switching to a more suit-

---

### Musk oil perfume

'Dried secretion painfully obtained from musk deer, beaver, muskrat, civet cat, and otter genitals. Wild cats are kept captive in cages in horrible conditions and are whipped around the genitals to produce the scent; beavers are trapped; deer are shot.'[1]

Synthetic alternatives to animal musks are available; however some perfume companies choose to use the real thing. Civet musk, for example, is still commonly used because the cats can be farmed. A 1999 World Society for the Protection of Animals investigation found that some top perfumeries, such as Chanel, Lancôme and Cartier, used civet musk despite the existence of alternatives.[2] ■

Sources: 1 www.caringconsumer.com/ingredientslist 2 World Society for the Protection of Animals, www.wspa-international.org

able breed, keeping the sheep clean, monitoring them closely during blowfly season, de-worming regularly to prevent diarrhea, or setting blowfly traps.[14]

## Cruel and inefficient

However, the most commonly used method to prevent blowfly infestation is 'mulesing'. This involves cutting off the skin around a sheep's tail and genitals so that when the skin grows back it will be smooth and less susceptible to blowfly larvae. 'Mulesing' is done without anesthetic and the resulting wound often gets infected. If it festers, the wound will attract the very parasite it is supposed to prevent thus making 'mulesing' a cruel and inefficient way to deal with the problem.[4] However sheep farmers do not want to have to pay extra staff required to monitor their thousands of sheep to prevent blowfly infestations.[14]

Sheep are subjected to many of the same procedures as other farm animals – they have their tails and ears docked, their teeth ground down, and are castrated, all without anesthetic. In the wool industry, sheep – like dairy cattle – are slaughtered when they become less productive. According to the Australian Law Reform Society, every year the country's sheep are subjected to 50 million procedures that would be considered cruel if done on pets.[4]

The majority of Australian sheep are exported when they start to produce low quality wool, because there isn't a large market for mutton (older sheep meat) at home. Every year, 7 million sheep are shipped to the Middle East, where they are ritually slaughtered (bled to death while conscious). Transport ships have up to 14 decks and can transport 125,000 sheep at a time. The mortality rate for Australian sheep exported to the Middle East is staggering – 18 per cent die due to overcrowding and poor ventilation and cooling systems.[13] In disasters at sea, tens of thousands of animals have died at once. In 2002, 14,500 died of heat stress during transit.[7]

Animal activists have been fairly successful in convincing the public that commercially trapped and farmed fur is cruel. A total of 88 countries have now banned the leghold trap for causing excessive suffering.[3] In 1995, the EU banned the imports of fur trapped this way and in 1997 Russia and Canada agreed to implement a ban on the trap.[4] The US however continues to use it. Thanks to the campaigning by activists, the UK, Austria and the Netherlands have banned fur farming altogether. This sets an important precedent because the majority of fur has been farmed in Europe. While the sale of furs has increased since the 1990s, it is nowhere near as popular as it once was. The majority of fur trim on parkas, for example, is still synthetic.

## Challenges ahead

The AR movement has been much less successful in convincing the public to avoid leather and wool. Many people see these as essential commodities and as the logical replacements for fur garments. However, some progress has been made. There is now a wide variety of leather and wool alternatives – many look and feel natural, and are even breathable. Because of the way leather and fur are produced, most vegans and some vegetarians avoid them.

Hundreds of retailers around the world sell shoes, jackets, belts, sweaters, and handbags that are made from animal-free materials. Toyota and Mercedes have even started producing automobiles with faux leather interiors. Campaigning by AR groups has also prompted many mainstream retailers to refuse Indian leather. Nearly 40 companies – including Gap, Nike and Gucci – have agreed to the boycott.[7] However, large discount chains, like Wal-Mart and K-Mart continue to buy Indian leather because it is some of the cheapest on the market.[15] Similarly, some retailers, such as New Look and J Crew, have stopped buying wool from producers who 'mules' their sheep. PETA is encouraging the public to boycott all Australian wool until producers agree to stop 'mulesing' and exporting live animals overseas.

**1** Interview with S Kumar, Humane Educator for People for the Ethical Treatment of Animals, 2005. **2** '"Democratization" of Fur', *Fur World*, 29 April 2002. **3** Coalition to Abolish the Fur Trade, www.caft.org.uk **4** Tom Regan, *Empty Cages* (Rowman and Littlefield, 2004). **5** 'Humans and Other Animals – The Facts', *New Internationalist* No 215, January 1991. **6** George Wenzel, *Animal Rights, Human Wrongs* (University of Toronto Press, 1991) **7** People For the Ethical Treatment of Animals, www.peta.org **8** Charlotte Montgomery, *Blood Relations* (Between the Lines, 2000) **9** Robert Garner, *Animals, Politics and Morality* (Manchester University Press, 1993) **10** *The New York Times*, 19 May 2000. **11** 'The Leather Global Value Chain and the World Leather Footwear Market', www.factbook.net/leather **12** Action for Animals, 'What's Wrong with Leather?' (pamphlet). **13** Action for Animals, 'What's Wrong with Wool?' (pamphlet). **14** Ingrid Newkirk, 'On the Front Line of the Sheep Wars', *Animal Talk*, Winter 2005. **15** *The New York Times*, 24 December 2000.

# 7 How hurting animals also hurts people

*'Nothing will benefit human health and increase chances for survival of life on Earth as much as the evolution to a vegetarian diet.'*
     – ALBERT EINSTEIN (1879-1955), PHYSICIST

**A vast corporate machinery profits greatly from the exploitation of animals and the world's consumption of animal products. People too, whether workers in factory farms or meat-eaters, are being harmed by the animal economy.**

WE HAVE SEEN in previous chapters how corporate consolidation and globalization has increased the suffering of animals. However, the same economic processes also hurt people. In fact, they have subjugated the majority of both human and non-human interests to the whims of the market, and a handful of powerful corporate interests. So-called 'market forces', which result in the gross mistreatment of animals to maximize profits, also justify the exploitation of people. The majority of corporations view both humans and animals as economic units, instead of living creatures. Many do not consider either human or animal lives as inherently valuable; rather their worth is based on their ability to produce goods or turn a profit. Just as animals' interests are not a part of the economic equation, neither are the interests of the world's most vulnerable people. Free-market global capitalism prioritizes profit over life. While some people are concerned that a focus on animal rights detracts from the important issue of human rights, animal and human economic exploitation is, in fact, a part of the same continuum. The free market obsession with the 'bottom line' has resulted in a basic

## Animals and people

devaluation of all life on the planet, including human life. Therefore, resisting the corporate agenda not only helps animals, but people as well.

### Animal foods industry

The meat, dairy and egg industries are responsible for the majority of direct and intentional animal suffering. As discussed in chapter 5, over 10 billion animals are killed every year for human consumption. But how do these industries affect people? Some would argue that they provide an essential service by raising and preparing food for people to eat. However, animal agriculture causes a great deal of both direct and indirect human suffering.

First of all, those responsible for the actual raising and slaughtering of food animals are some of the most exploited workers in the world. While farming has always been hard work, it now involves more occupational hazards. Instead of having a stake in their work, people employed at factory farms are paid the minimum wage to tend to animals owned by a distant corporation. Because such farming involves crowding animals into small spaces, often indoors, farm workers are exposed to dangerous chemicals. Cattle workers for example are exposed to pesticides because the beasts in feedlots are routinely sprayed as insects are drawn to their manure. Hog and chicken workers are exposed to dangerous levels of ammonia from livestock manure. A study at the University of Melbourne in Australia found that 70 per cent of chicken farm workers have chronic sore eyes, 30 per cent have regular coughing, and 15 per cent have asthma and chronic bronchitis.[1] Factory farm workers are also expected to deal with huge quantities of feces, which often contain dangerous bacteria, as well as with diseased, dying and dead animals.

Conditions in slaughterhouses are even worse. Injury rates are extremely high because workers are expected to dismember animals so quickly. In the US, the injury rate in the meat packing industry is three times the national average.[2] Meat-packing companies often recruit the most vulnerable sector of society – migrant workers – so they can save on labor costs. Many slaughterhouse workers are poor, illiterate and afraid of deportation. Managers prey on these weaknesses and routinely discourage injured workers from reporting accidents or seeking compensation.[2] Human Rights Watch has declared that North American slaughterhouses 'systematically violate human rights'.[3] However the industry has made little effort to improve safety standards and work conditions.

The corporations that dominate livestock production are very powerful economic interests. Because they control so many jobs in depressed rural areas, they have tremendous lobbying power with local and national governments. As a result, they have influence over government recommendations on diet.

*Canada's Food Guide to Healthy Eating* is only one example of a government-sponsored brochure to instruct the public on diet. While the *Guide* may be about nutrition, it is not actually compiled by doctors or nutritionists, but rather by representatives of the food and agricultural industries.[4] The emphasis on meat, eggs and dairy in the pamphlet is the work of well-organized lobbying efforts and is an essential marketing strategy for livestock producers. North Americans have been taught that a large amount of animal protein is essential to a well-balanced diet. In fact, North Americans are so obsessed with animal protein that it has been estimated that up to a million poor Americans buy pet food to supplement their diet.[5]

## Animal fats
However, increasingly doctors and nutritionists are concerned by the levels of animal fats and proteins that people eat. They are discovering more and more links

between the consumption of large amounts of animal foods and the incidence of diseases such as cancer, heart disease, stroke, diabetes and obesity. People who eat meat regularly are 50 per cent more likely to die of heart disease, have triple the blood pressure levels[6], and 20 per cent higher cholesterol levels, than vegetarians.[7] Studies also have shown that in countries where people eat relatively few animal products, the occurrence of such diseases is much lower. Moreover in

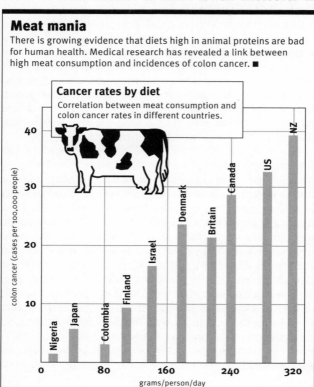

### Meat mania

There is growing evidence that diets high in animal proteins are bad for human health. Medical research has revealed a link between high meat consumption and incidences of colon cancer. ■

**Cancer rates by diet**
Correlation between meat consumption and colon cancer rates in different countries.

*colon cancer (cases per 100,000 people)*

*grams/person/day*

Source: National Cancer Institute, http://epi.grants.cancer.gov/ResPort/diet.html

countries that have recently adopted a more Western diet, like Japan, the rates of cancer, heart disease and diabetes have skyrocketed.[2]

Yet the meat, egg and dairy industries continue to insist, with government support, that people need to eat animal products every day to stay healthy.

Women, in particular, are encouraged to consume large amounts of dairy products (3-4 servings a day) for the calcium, to stave off osteoporosis. However, the high levels of protein in dairy products (cow's milk has three times as much protein as human milk) actually make it more difficult for the body to absorb calcium, and the rate of osteoporosis is highest in countries where people consume the most dairy. In China, for example, where dairy products are almost never eaten, osteoporosis is uncommon.[8] Diets rich in soy, nuts and green vegetables are actually more efficient at delivering calcium to the human body than dairy products.

## Bacterial infections

Meat that is industrially produced is particularly dangerous to human health. *E coli* and *salmonella* are the most common bacteria in factory farmed meat. *E coli* is found in cows' stomachs. When cattle are fattened in overcrowded feedlots, they often live in puddles of manure. Their feed and water is also commonly contaminated with feces. If any of the feces contains *E coli*, the cattle catch it. In the summertime, 50 per cent of cattle in feedlots have *E coli*. Because of the fast pace of slaughterhouse regimes, workers sometimes cut open a cow's bowels by mistake and feces splatters the carcass. If the cow has *E coli*, it gets into the meat supply. One cow with this bacterium can potentially contaminate 32,000 pounds of ground meat.[2] The infection generally causes bloody diarrhea and fever but it can also kill people. There have been hundreds of deaths from *E coli* in the US alone.

## Animals and people

*Salmonella* is the most common food-borne illness. Some 80 per cent of chicken meat is contaminated with it because factory chickens live in crowded cages, covered in feces and surrounded by corpses.[7] Eggs are also frequently affected. However, because chicken manure and by-products are also fed to other livestock, *salmonella* contaminates other meats as well. Every year in the US, there are 1.4 million cases of *salmonella* and some 500 deaths.[2] In addition, there are an estimated 310,000 cases in Britain; 160,000 in Canada; 102,000 in Australia and a whopping 6.6 million in China.[9] Because the majority of meat produced comes from animals that are sick and overcrowded in factory farms, 'it has been suggested that a piece of raw meat should be treated with the same degree of care in the kitchen as a piece of raw sewage'.[7]

## Mastitis

Factory farmed dairy products can be tainted as well. Anywhere from 30 per cent to 60 per cent of such dairy cattle are infected with mastitis,[10] which can be caused by 150 different bacteria. It causes painful swelling of the udder as well as discharge. Almost all commercially produced milk contains pus and blood that is sucked out with the milk from infected cows. The industry currently allows a content of 200 million pus cells per liter of milk.[11] The pus from mastitis contains the bacteria that caused the infection, so contaminated milk can contain *E coli*, for example, or paratuberculosis, which has been linked to Crohn's disease in humans.[12] Factory farmed dairy cows are treated with antibiotics to keep mastitis levels down. These antibiotics show up in their milk and when ingested, can lead to resistances in humans (antibiotics in meat have the same effect).[7] Organic milk farmers aren't allowed to use antibiotics and so they have to make sure their cows don't develop mastitis. Cows that are raised organically have access to cleaner bedding, more space and higher quality diets, which reduces their likelihood of developing the infection.

## Growth hormones

The use of bovine growth hormone, which dramatically increases a cow's milk yield, has led to increased mastitis in cows. Recombinant Bovine Growth Hormone (rBGH)-treated cows have a 79 per cent chance of developing the infection and their milk contains 19 per cent more pus and blood. Because of this susceptibility to the infection, the cows need to be given higher levels of antibiotics to stave off mastitis, which later turns up in their milk. rBGH, manufactured by US corporation Monsanto, has also been linked to cancer.[13] Luckily, the EU, Canada, Australia, New Zealand and Japan have banned the use of bovine growth hormones. However they are widely used in the US.

Scientists are increasingly concerned about a phenomenon called bio-accumulation, whereby toxins are stored in fatty tissue and become more concentrated as they go up the food chain. Because humans are at the top of the food chain, scientists are concerned that we are exposed to highly concentrated chemicals through the food we eat. Bio-accumulation mostly has been studied in fish that are exposed to pollution. Small fish that eat at the bottom of the food chain (plants and algae) have the lowest level of toxins, whereas those who eat other fish have higher levels depending on where they are in the food chain. When humans, or other animals, eat the large fish that are at the top of the aquatic food chain, such as halibut, tuna and salmon, they are exposing themselves to a higher concentration of chemicals than found in the environment.

The same phenomenon occurs with livestock. Food animals (including farmed fish) are fed a high protein diet so that they will gain weight quickly. Much of this protein is derived from animal parts. Because the animals that end up in feed have either eaten grain that is heavily laced with pesticides, or have come from polluted oceans, their bodies already contain a higher level of toxins. When livestock are fed these animal proteins (as well as more grain treated with pesticides), the toxins they ingest accumulate in their fatty tissue. When humans eat this, the toxins become even more concentrated in our bodies.

The US-based Sierra Club, and many other environmental organizations, encourages the public to eat lower down on the food chain, and consume less animal fat, to avoid ingesting highly concentrated chemicals.[14] Conventional agricultural practices, which encourage large-scale pesticide use and the feeding of animal protein to herbivores, are compounding the risks of pollution.

## A question of resources

Social and environmental justice activists also have problems with the way meat is produced. One major problem is that the meat industry is contributing to food scarcity. Instead of growing subsistence crops, many developing nations either intensively raise animals for Western consumption or grow grain to feed livestock in the West. '[T]he people who need food most are using their land.... to feed the meat-eating habits of those who have quite enough food already,' writes Mark Gold in the *New Internationalist* magazine.[15] In addition, most of the cereals grown in the West are used to feed livestock. The grains and soy used in cattle fodder in the US alone could feed over one billion people, and world hunger could be alleviated if North Americans reduced their meat consumption by only 10 per cent (assuming the grain saved was made available to the poor).[6]

Another problem is that many of the planet's natural ecosystems and resources are being destroyed by livestock operations. Grazing is the number one cause of deforestation and species loss. For every quarter pound (0.1 kg) burger made by a fast-food restaurant, 55 square feet (5.1 square meters) of land is used. This means that for every 'quarter-pounder', 1,102 pounds (500 kg) of wildlife and saplings are destroyed.[7] Brazilian beef production for the fast food industry is one of the leading causes of the destruction of the Amazon.

It also takes vastly more fossil fuel and water to produce meat as opposed to plant-based proteins. For example, to produce a single hamburger patty requires as much fossil fuel as needed to drive a car 20 miles (32 km). Likewise, it takes 2,500 gallons (9,464 liters) of water to produce one pound (0.45 kg) of beef while it takes only 25 gallons (95 liters) to produce one pound (0.45 kg) of wheat.[16] Many environmentalists believe that the meat industry is wasting precious resources.

## Meat and the environment

Livestock rearing also results in a huge amount of waste matter. Factory-farmed animals produce 500 million tons of manure every day. This is 130 times more feces than is provided by the US population.[16] Most animal manure is 20-40 times more potent than human waste, which means that it is much more harmful once it leaches into water systems. Around 60 per cent of water pollution in the US is caused by agricultural waste (which includes run-off from agro-chemicals).[6] The methane gas produced by the billions of food animals also significantly contributes to global warming. Methane gas is the second worst greenhouse gas, and 27 per cent of it is produced by livestock.[6] Scientist David Suzuki suggests that reducing meat consumption significantly helps decrease global warming.[17]

The way animal agriculture is currently practiced is unsustainable for the planet and bad for people. Not only are animal activists outraged at the way animals are treated in factory farms, but social, consumer and environmental advocates condemn this intensive rearing for its exploitation of people and natural resources.

## Leather industry

Many people, including vegetarians, wear leather because they believe it is better for the environment than synthetic products. Some leather manufacturers even market their products as eco-friendly, suggesting that they will biodegrade quickly once discarded. If people wore untreated leather, this would be true. However, the leather we wear goes through intensive processing to prevent it from biodegrading while we are wearing it. It is commonly treated with formaldehyde, coal-tar derivatives and the highly toxic chromium. The tanning industry is a heavy polluter – run-off has been known to taint water supplies. Lead, cyanide and formaldehyde have all been found in groundwater near tanning works. Pollution from this industry has been linked to cancer – residents living near a facility in Kentucky had a leukemia rate five times the US national average.[16]

Tannery workers, exposed to higher concentrations of chemicals, are particularly prone to lung and sinus cancer. A study of such workers in Italy and Sweden found that they had cancer rates between 20-50 per cent above what experts expected.[16] Because of the health and safety risks associated with tanning, the majority of factories have moved to developing countries where labor and environmental standards are often lower. Run-off from tanneries throughout the South is contaminating water supplies, poisoning crops and livestock and making local residents sick.

Just as leather is processed in the developing world, it is manufactured into goods there as well. Approximately 80 per cent of garments, including shoes and handbags, are made in sweatshops.[18] Sweatshop workers, mostly women, are exploited. Many governments are willing to turn a blind eye to the labor conditions in sweatshops in order to attract investment to their countries and increase exports.[19] 'Sweated' workers are given short-term contracts, forced to work long hours in terrible conditions. They are often paid just pennies per hour, and are denied sick and maternity leave. While clothing workers frequently have respiratory infections from the lint in the cloth they work with, shoe workers are exposed to toxic chemicals used to treat, dye and glue shoes.

## Sweatshops

Sweatshops that make shoes are concentrated in Asia, perhaps because Asia supplies the bulk of the world's leather. Most shoes are made in China, which has few labor standards and a bad human rights record. Chinese shoe-workers are expected to work 12-hour shifts and only get two to four vacation days a month. They are paid as little as $30 a month and receive no benefits. One of the most dangerous aspects of the job is exposure to glue containing benzene. This can cause leukemia and anemia, and has been banned in Europe and the US but continues to be used in countries that don't have stringent health and environmental laws. Shoe factories commonly lack basic ventilation and safety equipment, such as masks, gloves and goggles. Employees frequently suffer from headaches, dizziness and skin irritation. There have even been reports of shoe workers dying from inhaling toxic fumes. Child labor is common in Chinese shoe factories, many of which are subcontractors for companies such Nike, Reebok and Adidas, and the Government actively represses union organizing in all its garment factories.[20]

The shoes, sneakers, bags and belts we wear every day not only involve suffering for the animals killed for their hides, but also for tannery and garment workers. These goods, which are manufactured for Western markets, are made in complete violation of Western labor and environmental, not to mention animal welfare, laws.

## Drug and product testing

Animal tests are notoriously inaccurate when it comes to determining side effects in humans.[21] But because they are the dominant scientific testing model, huge numbers of dangerous medications and products go on the market. In 1998, the *Journal of the American Medical Association* reported that adverse reactions to medication are the fourth leading cause of death in the US. Approximately 15 per cent of all hospital admissions are prompted by negative side effects to medicines. These adverse reactions are to drugs that have been screened through animal tests and not deemed a threat to human health.[22]

By the late 19th century, scientists had started to realize that animal tests often could not be repli-

---

### Military experiments

Most countries use animals to test their military technology. Every year several hundred thousand animals are subjected to military experiments. The US Department of Defense uses more than 300,000 animals annually, which costs taxpayers $100 million. One of the purposes of this research is to test weapons that will potentially be used on humans. Dogs, cats, pigs and monkeys are exposed to nuclear radiation, nerve gas, and various chemical and bacterial agents. They are also burned, maimed and shot with guns and missiles so that governments can develop the most lethal weapons possible. ∎

Source: In Defense of Animals, www.idaus.org

---

cated in humans. Since this time, the inaccuracy of animal testing has been proven over and over again. Thousands of medications have been pulled from the market for causing harm to humans. Isuprel, an asthma drug, killed 3,500 people in Britain alone, despite extensive toxicology tests on animals. The drug Primacor was also taken off the market because while it improved circulation in the heart, it also increased deaths in humans by 30 per cent.

Two pharmaceutical companies were included in 2004's 'Ten Worst Corporations' list produced by *Multinational Monitor* because they manufactured drugs that were harmful to humans. GlaxoSmithKline produced the anti-depressant Paxil, which was found to cause increased suicide in youth, and Merck produced the painkiller Vioxx, which caused 88,000-139,000 heart attacks and 35,000-55,000 deaths in the US alone. USDA's Dr David Graham called the sale of Vioxx 'maybe the single greatest drug-safety catastrophe in the history of this country'.[23]

The same problem exists with other products, including food additives, pesticides and industrial chemicals. Even though many animals are not susceptible to the same forms of cancer as humans, carcinogenic products often are approved for sale based on animal tests. For example, the cancer-causing effects of asbestos were noticed in humans at the beginning of the 20th century. But because asbestos didn't lead to cancer in animals, it remained on the market for decades.[22] Asbestos wasn't regulated at all until 1969 in Britain and 1971 in the US and wasn't deemed toxic until the 1980s.

The pesticide DDT is another dangerous chemical that was widely used for many years before eventually being pulled from the market. Currently scientists are worried that flame retardants containing methylbromide may also be toxic to humans despite the fact that they've been on the market for years and have now become highly concentrated in human breast milk.[24]

Likewise, potentially beneficial products can be kept off the market because of animal tests. Penicillin, the world's leading antibiotic, would never have been developed if Sir Alexander Fleming had relied on animal tests because it killed the guinea pigs he tested it on.[25] Fleming later stated that the entire field of antibiotics would never have been developed if animal testing had been common in the 1940s.[22] Likewise, insulin causes deformities in mice and rats but is extremely beneficial to humans. Many other important drugs have been developed solely through patient observation and *in vitro* tests, such as aspirin, morphine, digitalis (for heart disease), and varatum alkaloids (for blood pressure).[21]

### Failing the test

For years, scientists have been warning that animal tests are unreliable. Some companies have started to listen. As discussed in chapter 6, several cosmetics firms have stopped using animal tests. The Anglo-American company Asterand, plc. only uses human tissue (discarded from operations) for its drug tests.[26] However, despite the harm that it can cause humans, animal experimentation is still the norm for medical research and product testing; it is currently the cheapest and easiest research model. The infrastructure and technology for animal testing is well established in labs. Other models (such as human studies and *in vitro* testing) have been ignored for years and pharmaceutical and chemical companies have little incentive to invest in new research technologies or change their practices. Some critics believe that these industries are resistant to change partly because more accurate tests would mean fewer products would be approved for sale. As it stands, companies can still make millions before a dangerous product is pulled from the market.

For example, sales from Vioxx reached $2 billion before it was deemed unsafe.[27] Pharmaceuticals are the most profitable industry in the world. Perhaps this is because it is willing to put profits above human health.

## The benefits of humane education

The mentality that leads to animal abuse is similar to that which leads to violence towards humans. Early philosophers, such as Aristotle and Aquinas, believed that animals should be protected from cruelty not because they possessed moral rights, but rather because allowing cruelty toward them would encourage people to be cruel to each other as well. Studies have shown that these philosophers were right: people are who violent to animals tend to be violent to people as well. According to the FBI, many violent criminals, such as serial rapists and murderers, have a history of cruelty toward animals.[16] Most of the well-known serial killers of this century 'practiced' on animals before turning on people.[28]

Some people consider it 'normal' for children, particularly boys, to torture animals. However back in 1905, Freud suggested that clinicians should pay close attention to children who are cruel to animals.[28] Increasingly experts are seeing the connection between animal abuse and violence. According to a study conducted by Cornell University, there is 'a consensus... among psychologists...that cruelty to animals is one of the best examples of the continuity of psychological disturbances from childhood to adulthood'. Animal abuse is a sign of serious mental disturbance. Anthropologist Margaret Mead noted: 'One of the most dangerous things that can happen to a child is to kill or torture an animal and get away with it.'[16]

There also seems to be a connection between animal abuse and domestic abuse. Many battered women and children have reported that the family pet was the first victim of violence. And some children who are exposed to violence emulate the behavior they see by hurting the family pet. The correlation between these types of abuse is so strong that police in the US and the UK are working with vets and animal control officers to detect cases.[28]

## Violence

Violence of any kind can lead to a dangerous cycle. Children who are taught to care for animals and respect life in general are more likely to be nurturing and kind to humans. Many people, particularly men, are programmed to turn off their emotions when confronted with animal suffering. As Richard Ryder has argued, this 'cult of machismo' has enabled some men to differentiate themselves from women and children, which society tends to view as 'weak'.[29] By being callous about animal suffering, some men may be asserting their 'masculinity,' but at what cost? Studies consistently indicate that disregard for animal life is all too often linked to a similar disregard for human life. Psychologists have concluded that 'the evolution of more gentle and benign relationships in human society might... be enhanced by our promotion of a more positive and nurturing ethic between children and animals.'[16]

Much animal suffering is directly connected to human suffering. The industries that exploit the most animals, such as the meat, leather and pharmaceutical industries, have no qualms about exploiting people as well. These industries repeatedly have shown blatant disregard for human wellbeing. This shouldn't be surprising considering that study after study has shown that humans who are unable to empathize with animals are less able to empathize with humans as well. Deliberate cruelty to animals is an early indicator of lack of empathy and lack of empathy is a primary component of psychopathy. It makes sense that the corporations that are deliberately cruel to huge numbers of animals also have little regard for human well being. In fact Mark Achbar and Joel Bakan, makers of the film *The Corporation*, suggest that corporations are 'prototypical psychopath[s]' because they show 'callous unconcern for the feelings of others'.[30] Unfortunately, the corporate ethic dominates our global economic system, often at the expense of living things, both animal and human.

**1** Peter Singer, *Animal Liberation* 3rd edition (Pimlico, 1995). **2** Eric Schlosser, *Fast Food Nation* (Perennial, 2001). **3** *The New York Times*, 6 February 2005. **4** *The Globe and Mail*, 12 March 2005. **5** Robert Garner, *Animals, Politics and Morality* (Manchester University Press, 1993). **6** Animal Place, www.animal-place.org **7** Gayle Hardy, 'Prime Cut', *New Internationalist* No 215, January 1991. **8** Michael Klaper, MD, *A Diet for All Reasons* (documentary). **9** 'Statistics by Country for Salmonella Food Poisoning', www.wrongdiagnosis.com **10** Animal Aid, www.animalaid.org.uk **11** Harold Brown, Farm Sanctuary Campaigner, 'What's Wrong with Free-range and Organic', lecture at Toronto Animal Rights Society, 2005. **12** I Murray 'Crohn's Linked To Bacteria In Milk' *The Times* (London), January 25, 2000. **13** Environmental Research Foundation, www.ejnet.org **14** Sierra Club of Canada, *Scan Special Issue: Pesticides*, April 2005. **15** Mark Gold, 'On the Meat-hook', *New Internationalist* No 215, January 1991. **16** People for the Ethical Treatment of Animals, www.peta.org **17** David Suzuki Foundation, www.davidsuzuki.org **18** Behind the Label, www.behindthelabel.org **19** Oxfam, www.oxfam.org **20** Corpwatch, www.corpwatch.org **21** Robert Sharpe, *The Cruel Deception* (Thorsons Publishing, 1988). **22** CR Greek, MD and JS Greek, DVM, *Sacred Cows and Golden Geese* (Continuum, 2000). **23** Canadian Center for Policy Alternatives, *CCPA Monitor*, April 2005. **24** British Union for the Abolition of Vivisection, www.buav.org **25** 'Humans and Other Animals – The Facts', *New Internationalist* No 215, January 1991. **26** Matthew Scully, *Dominion* (St Martin's Press, 2002). **27** *The Globe and Mail*, 19 February 2005. **28** Lynda Stoner, 'The Cycle of Violence', www.animal-lib.org.au **29** Richard Ryder, *The Political Animal* (McFarland, 1998). **30** Mark Achbar and Joel Bakan, *The Corporation* (documentary), Zeitgeist Films, 2004.

# 8 Comparative treatment of animals

*'The human race is challenged more than ever before to demonstrate our mastery, not over nature, but of ourselves.'*

– RACHEL CARSON (1907-1964), BIOLOGIST

**Some countries and local governments are leading the way in terms of instituting legal recognition of animal rights and providing important protections. Much of the world, however, is still lagging behind.**

EUROPEAN COUNTRIES OFFER the most legal protection to animals. In 1997 the EU acknowledged that mammals are sentient creatures and that laws governing their use need to reflect this important fact.[1] While widespread industrial animal-use continues on a daily basis, the EU has attempted to regulate farming and animal testing in order to minimize pain and distress. Animal welfare, and even animal rights, has broad popular support in many European countries. The European Community has taken significant steps in reducing animal suffering, albeit without challenging the notion of animal use.

Industrialized countries outside Europe do not have nearly such well-developed animal welfare laws. Currently Eastern and Southern European countries that belong to the EU are working with that body to improve their standards.

Many former Soviet countries are just now developing their first animal welfare laws. As these countries do not have extensive animal research programs, the major areas of concern are the farming and entertainment industries, as well as the treatment of companion animals.

Cruelty to animals is particularly a problem in Southern Europe, where blood sports and the extermination of strays are still common.[1] Australia and New Zealand have fairly good regulations in place

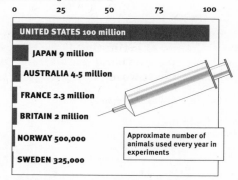

## Testing times

Over 100 million animals are used annually and subsequently killed in experiments, mostly in universities, pharmaceutical companies, and commercial testing facilities. ■

| 0 | 25 | 50 | 75 | 100 |

**UNITED STATES 100 million**

**JAPAN 9 million**

**AUSTRALIA 4.5 million**

**FRANCE 2.3 million**

**BRITAIN 2 million**

**NORWAY 500,000**

**SWEDEN 325,000**

Approximate number of animals used every year in experiments

Sources: European Biomedical Association, www.ebra.org/stats/; US Department of Agriculture (USDA); 'Animals in Scientific Procedures: Regulations in Japan', www.publications.parliament.uk; AESOP Project, www.aesop-project.org; M Budkie, 'Rising Tide of Animal Experimentation', www.all-creatures.org; Professor Adrian Smith, 'The Use of Research Animals in Norway', http://oslovet.veths.no/info; www.humanecharities.org.au.

to monitor animal experiments, and protect pets. Both countries have very strong laws to preserve wild native species; however they are controversial because they advocate the mass killing of invasive mammals (such as possums). In addition, because agricultural interests are quite strong in both countries, regulations regarding the treatment of farm animals are weak. Australia, for example, has excluded poultry from animal welfare laws and both countries allow the overseas transport of live animals.

### North America

In general, North America does not have nearly such strong animal welfare laws as Europe, Australia and New Zealand. The US has notoriously inadequate animal welfare standards, compared with

## Primate blues

Primates are our closest relatives in the animal kingdom, sharing nearly 99 per cent of our DNA, our ability to use tools, form complex social relationships and even use language – and yet ironically it is those qualities which make them prime candidates for scientific experiments. ■

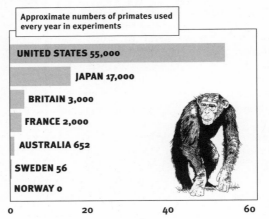

**Approximate numbers of primates used every year in experiments**

UNITED STATES 55,000

JAPAN 17,000

BRITAIN 3,000

FRANCE 2,000

AUSTRALIA 652

SWEDEN 56

NORWAY 0

0          20          40          60

Sources: European Biomedical Association, www.ebra.org/stats/; US Department of Agriculture (USDA); 'Animals in Scientific Procedures: Regulations in Japan', www.publications.parliament.uk; AESOP Project, www.aesop-project.org; M Budkie, 'Rising Tide of Animal Experimentation', www.all-creatures.org; Professor Adrian Smith, 'The Use of Research Animals in Norway', http://oslovet.veths.no/info; www.humanecharities.org.au.

other developed nations. Relatively speaking, the US by far exploits the largest number of animals. Literally billions of animals are killed there every year for sport, food, and scientific experiments. US animal welfare law is weak on most forms of animal use, and many creatures – like rodents, reptiles, fish and birds – are excluded altogether from the law.

The farming and scientific communities are largely left to regulate their own practices. European restrictions on the most painful farming and scientific procedures are absent from US laws. While some individual US states have made progress on animal welfare, the nation as a whole lags far behind the rest of the Western world. Princeton University ethicist Peter Singer believes that this is the case because, despite the strength of the AR movement, business interests are entrenched in the American political system.[1]

Canada too is behind on animal welfare standards. Like in the US, the scientific and farming communities regulate themselves without government interference.[2] The Canadian Animal Welfare Act has not been updated since the 19th century and therefore does not address many of the concerns present in a modern industrial society.

## Japan

Japan has some of the worst animal welfare standards. While there is an animal welfare act, it has no practical value. Experiments on animals are unregulated, and many extremely painful tests that have been banned in many countries are still conducted in Japan.[1] While the Government recently agreed to regulate conditions in zoos, circuses, pet stores and breeding facilities, there have been few efforts to enforce standards. Animals in these places continue to face some of the worst conditions in the industrialized world.

Factory farming is also widespread and little has been done to regulate conditions for livestock. The nation has also been criticized for its refusal to protect endangered species. The ivory trade is flourishing and the Government insists on its right to hunt endangered whales.[3] In fact whale meat was recently reintroduced into the school lunch program,[4] which suggests little interest in changing whaling practices.

Because the country falls badly behind the standards of the rest of the industrialized world, 100 Japanese animal welfare/rights groups (as well as many international organizations) are currently lobbying the Government to reform its archaic laws.

## Latin America

Countries that suffer from poverty, socio-political instability and conflict have fewer resources to put towards safeguarding animals. Nonetheless, many Southern countries have implemented laws to protect animals. Several Latin American countries, including Brazil, Colombia, Peru, Mexico and Argentina, have done so. Brazil has one of the most sophisticated animal welfare acts in the region. The State allows the representation of animal interests in court, cockfighting and bullfighting are illegal, marine animals cannot be kept in captivity, and animal experiments conducted without anesthetic are forbidden. Brazil also has strong conservation laws, which make it illegal to mistreat wild animals.[5]

There also is a widespread movement in Latin America to humanely control stray pet populations. Brazil, Argentina, Uruguay and Costa Rica have implemented spay/neuter and vaccination programs with the goal of ending the killing of stray cats and dogs.[6]

## Asia

Asian countries have a bad reputation among AR activists in terms of animal treatment. Practices like raising cats and dogs for meat, selling live animals in markets, and the use of animal parts in traditional medicines, are of concern to animal activists.

Animal welfare laws still are not common in the region. However, some countries are starting to move toward the legal protection of animals. Taiwan and the Philippines enacted their first animal welfare laws in 1998. Both countries have established humane slaughter regulations, and, controversially, offer some protection to cats and dogs. Taiwan has also made it illegal to fight or race any animals or use animals for gambling purposes.

Taiwan has also established an ethics committee to supervise animal experiments. In some respects, these animal laws are more far-reaching than US legislation. While China still conducts largely unregulated animal experiments, as discussed in chapter 3, the nation has taken some important steps toward protecting animals. The Government is under pressure to implement its first-ever animal welfare act. As well, a joint UN/Humane Society International project is currently underway to provide humane slaughter training for individuals from Asian and Pacific countries.[7]

## Africa

Because they are poor, most African countries have few resources to put towards protecting animals. Despite this obstacle, many have taken steps to protect endangered wildlife. Large wildlife preserves have been successfully established in countries like Kenya and Tanzania. While preventing poaching is more difficult in war-torn countries, like Zimbabwe, Angola and DR Congo, laws forbidding it do exist and local officials do their best to enforce them. Part of the problem is widespread economic insecurity throughout the continent.

Many rural people are poor with few employment opportunities. They turn to poaching to eke out a living, and either sell endangered animals on the black market or use their meat. In some African countries, efforts are being made to help local people participate in eco-tourism, so that they can profit from their country's wildlife without having to resort to hunting it. African countries are also making efforts to educate the public about the value of its wildlife, and animals in general.

In 2003, Swaziland and Mozambique implemented humane education programs into their public school curricula, in an effort to teach children to treat

## Comparative treatment

living things with respect.[8] South Africa has anti-cruelty laws which forbid the killing of pets, neglect or overwork of draft animals, and animal fighting.[9] Recently, the Government recognized that animals are sentient and made the commitment to treat both wild and domestic animals humanely.[8]

Animal welfare standards vary dramatically by region. It's easy to point fingers at the poorer nations that don't have comprehensive animal welfare laws – however protection laws don't necessarily save animals from exploitation. In fact, the richest Western countries which have the best welfare standards also carry out the vast majority of animal exploitation, because they have well-established farming, pharmaceutical and chemical industries. So while they may have progressive laws regarding animals, they nonetheless sanction widespread animal suffering.

### Animals in the Global South

Southern countries, on the other hand, may have less sophisticated animal welfare laws but in practice harm fewer animals – in large part because they consume fewer resources than Northerners.

For example, out of the 25 billion animals that are killed every year for food, only one billion are killed to feed people in the Global South.[7] Many of these animals are raised by local small farmers, who use non-intensive systems. Much of the Majority World cannot afford Northern agricultural technology, and the result is more sustainable and humane livestock operations.

In addition, while most animals raised in the North are killed within the first few months of their lives, animals in the South are kept much longer because they are considered very valuable. A chicken that can lay eggs, or a cow that can provide milk for several years is worth too much to be slaughtered for meat within a year or two. Draft animals are also widely

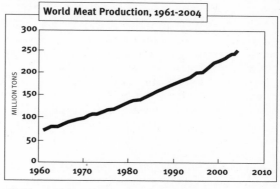

**Meat market**

Increasing global demand for meat is driving the industry and pushing producers to adopt more intensive 'factory farming' methods for rearing animals. ■

**World Meat Production, 1961-2004**

Sources: Worldwatch Institute, *Vital Signs 2005* (WW Norton & Company 2005); UN Food & Agriculture Organization (FAO).

used in less industrialized societies, and so animals have a function other than providing food. While the over-work and neglect of draft animals is a real problem, most people do their best to treat their stock well because these are essential to the household economy.[10]

The real danger for animals in the Global South comes from the infringement of Northern agricultural practices. As discussed in chapters 5 and 8, many US and European agri-businesses are taking advantage of lower environmental, labor, and animal welfare laws in the South, to establish factory farms. Industrial farming practices combined with the lack formal laws to protect animals, has resulted in widespread livestock abuse.

Animal protection groups, like the World Society for the Protection of Animals and CIWF are urging

---

## How trade laws hurt farm animals

When it comes to animal welfare, international trade laws usually recognize the lowest common denominator. In fact, 'current World Trade Organization rules... make it illegal to ban the import of animal products from countries on the basis that they are not produced in line with a state's own standards of animal welfare'.[1] This is becoming an issue for the EU, which has implemented a ban on battery cages and gestational crates. Countries that have lower welfare guidelines are now able to argue that their farm products are facing unfair trade restrictions because of higher European standards.[2] ■

Sources: 1 Compassion in World Farming, www.ciwf.org.uk
2 Pat Tohill, 'Industrial Animal Agriculture', Two Days of Thinking about Animals in Canada (conference), Brock University, 2005.

---

governments and international development agencies to preserve traditional farming systems in the Majority World.

Encouraging sustainable local farming practices, and generally educating the public about the value of living creatures will help improve animal welfare standards in the Majority World. However, the single most important step to achieving compassion for animals in the South is by protecting human rights and eliminating poverty. Until the majority of the world's population has access to enough food, fair wages, and political freedom, they will be unable to prioritize the interests of animals. People whose own basic needs are not being met cannot be expected to fight for animal rights. As it stands, widespread human poverty is a serious impediment to protecting animals.

### The need to improve standards

While it is important to fight for both human and animal rights in the South, concerned citizens should also focus on countries in the industrialized North that do not meet international welfare standards. Citizens should demand that their governments implement excellent welfare standards and even basic rights for the animals that they profit from. The US, Canada and Japan in particular, as three of the richest nations in the world, should be compelled to bring their standards into line with their European counterparts.

Animal rights activists should also resist corporate attempts to spread systemic animal abuse to the Majority World. Globalization has paved the way for double standards; a country can have excellent standards within its own borders but depend on goods and services from nations with less stringent guidelines. Until wealthy nations insist on universally enforcing production standards, and do not allow their own companies to ignore them abroad, animals will continue to be mercilessly exploited.

**1** Mark Gold, *Animal Century* (Jon Carpenter, 1998). **2** Charlotte Montgomery, *Blood Relations* (Between the Lines, 2000). **3** Alive, www.alive-net/english/ **4** *The Australian*, 2 May 2005, www.theaustralian.news.com.au **5** Lane Azevedo Clayton, 'Overview of Brazil's Legal Structure for Animal Issues', www.animal-law.info **6** Alice Cook, 'Animal Abuse: Legislation in North America and Latin America', Proceedings of the World Small Animal Veterinary Association, 2001, www.vin.com **7** Humane Society of the United States, www.hsus.org **8** Humane Education Trust, www.animal-voice.org **9** South African Animal Anti-Cruelty League, www.satis.co.za **10** 'Humans and Other Animals – The Facts', *New Internationalist* No 215, January 1991.

# 9 A practical guide to reducing animal suffering

*'To be a vegetarian is to disagree – to disagree with the course of things today. Starvation, world hunger, cruelty, waste, wars – we must make a statement against these things. Vegetarianism is my statement. And I think it's a strong one.'*
– ISAAC BASHEVIS SINGER (1902-1991), WRITER

DON'T BE OVERWHELMED! When confronted by the knowledge of widespread animal exploitation, people sometimes feel overwhelmed and helpless. Because animal exploitation is involved in many aspects of our day-to-day lives, it seems impossible to stop animal suffering. However, while one individual can't save all animals from human abuse, each of us does have the power to reduce animal suffering through our lifestyle and consumer choices. Here are some suggestions about how to make a difference.

## 1 Consume less
The most practical way we can help animals is to reduce our consumption of them. Like it or not, every item that we produce and use affects the world around us. Everything we buy requires raw materials and energy to produce.

The harvesting of these, and the pollution created by the mass production of consumer goods and foodstuffs, adversely impacts all living things by destroying and poisoning ecosystems. Currently, the human population is using 20 per cent more resources and energy than the earth can generate. And most of us in the industrialized world consume vastly more than we need.

If we don't stop, we will destroy the planet, and all creatures on it (including us).

## 2 Buy responsibly

We don't only need to consume less energy and manu-factured goods, we also have to make responsible choices. The production of items as basic as toilet paper, coffee and bananas, cotton clothing and plastic packaging results in the death of millions of animals every year. Nobody wants to give these things up, and luckily options are available that are more sustainable. Paper made from recycled fibers saves old-growth forests; organically grown and fairly traded bananas and coffee (shade grown in particular) spare countless birds and insects and help communities earn a decent wage; organic cotton clothing also spares birds, rodents and insects, and avoids polluting the rivers and lakes that wildlife and people depend on; recycled (and recyclable) plastic packaging prevents the extrac-tion of more fossil fuels, which destroy wildlife habi-tats and human communities and pollute the air.

There are countless ways to reduce your 'ecological footprint' and still enjoy life: such as composting and recycling, and buying locally produced and organic goods. To learn more about the human 'ecological footprint', see www.footprintnetwork.org. To calcu-late your own personal footprint, take the test at: www.mec.ca

## 3 Reduce the amount of animal protein in your diet

By far the largest number of animals mistreated and killed by humans are for food. Some activists choose not to eat any animal products because of this: they avoid all meat, fish, dairy and eggs. It is possible to live a healthy and active life on a vegan diet, if you are willing to take time to learn how to get all the nutrients your body needs. However, simply reduc-ing the amount of animal products in your diet is a step in the right direction both for animals and your health. Instead of having meat every day, experiment with lower-fat vegetarian substitutes such as beans, whole grains and tofu. And try using soy or rice milk in tea/coffee and baked goods. Giving up these things for one meal a day will save animal lives.

## 4 Buy free-range and organic products

Many activists avoid eating animal products. However, if you can't imagine life without meat, eggs and dairy, it's important to buy them from responsible local farmers who don't use intensive systems. Many small independent farms have much more humane practices than large factory farms, and free-range and organic systems are much better for animals. While humanely-raised animals will eventually be slaughtered, at least they are subjected to considerably less distress during their lives. Take the time to talk to the farmers and producers who you buy from to make sure that you are comfortable with their raising techniques and that their livestock are not shipped long distances before slaughter. Most grocery store chains are starting to stock free-range and organic products – but better yet check out your local farmers' market or health food store because they are more likely to have locally raised meat, eggs and dairy (which mean less stress for the animals and less pollution from transportation).

## 5 Be aware of hidden animal ingredients

Unfortunately, there are all sorts of hidden animal ingredients in many of the products we consume. These ingredients come from the by-products of factory farmed animals. Many baked goods contain an animal fat called glyceride, some maple syrups and molasses contain lard as an anti-foaming agent, brown and white sugar is refined using animal charcoal. Also watch for rennet, lactic acid, pepsin and gelatin in foods: all animal-derived. Cosmetics also use an array of animal products such as collagen, glycerin, elastin, and lanolin which are all from animal tissue. For a comprehensive list, see Tanya Barnard and Sarah Kramer, *The Garden of Vegan* (Arsenal Pulp Press, 2002). However animal byproducts are used only because mass scale factory farming makes them available very cheaply. If people consumed less meat, manufacturers would be forced to find alternatives.

### 6 Don't buy products tested on animals

Look for the cruelty-free rabbit icon on the products you buy. Unless they state otherwise, most commercial products are tested on animals. Luckily there are cruelty-free alternatives to most products, and they are becoming increasingly available in supermarkets. It's now easy to find cleaning and household products and personal care items that haven't been tested on animals. PETA has compiled an extension list of companies that do and do not test on animals (as well as ones that are adhering to a moratorium), and gives free copies to interested consumers (www.peta.org).

Beauty Without Cruelty cosmetics can be purchased via Animal Aid: www.animalaid.org.uk

### 7 Don't be a fashion victim

Leather and wool clothing are staples in most people's wardrobes. However, they involve a considerable degree of cruelty. In the last few years, excellent alternatives have been developed: sweaters come in a variety of materials and several companies manufacture high-quality leather-free shoes.

However even if you choose to wear leather and wool, there are other ways of reducing animal distress. First of all, buying second-hand sweaters, belts and handbags reduces waste and make use of existing products without causing any further animal suffering. Secondly, invest in a couple of well-made items that will last a long time, instead of buying lots of cheaper ones that will soon need to be replaced. Quality sweaters and leather goods that can be repaired will last several years. One of the biggest problems for animals is that fashions change frequently and clothing is made to be disposable. Once the 'season' is over, consumers are expected to buy new clothes in updated styles. Because of this, people end up buying many more things than they really need – and when it comes to leather and wool, it is at the expense of animals. So if you don't want to give up leather and wool, at least buy more responsibly. Choose 'classic' items that will not immediately go out of style and wear them until they're worn out. (One exception: for reasons discussed in chapter 8, avoid all merino wool).

### 8 Understand the needs of pets

Having pets can be a wonderful experience. However, it's important to choose ones that you are able to care for properly. Most experts believe that keeping exotic and caged pets (like reptiles, small rodents, birds and even fish) is cruel, even when owners have the best intentions. Many other types of pets – such as cats and dogs – do much better in human homes. Because of the pet overpopulation crisis and the cruelty involved in the pet store and pet breeding industry, it is better to adopt animals from shelters. Instead of supporting an unscrupulous industry, you will be saving an animal that might otherwise be destroyed.

Be sure to spay and neuter your pet, so there are no unwanted ones. Unfortunately most pet food is made from the factory farmed animals who have suffered the most – those who arrive at slaughterhouses either dead or dying. Most commercial pet food companies also conduct painful animal experiments to test their products. For these reasons, some animal advocates try to feed their pets vegetarian (and even vegan) diets. However, there are other ways to help reduce the suffering of animals used in the production of pet food, such as buying pet foods made from organic, free-range or even just human-grade meats. This will insure that producers do not profit from mistreating their livestock. Several of the companies that guarantee higher meat quality also guarantee that their products have not been tested on animals.

For information on vegetarian/vegan alternatives to petfood see: www.veggiepets.com

## 9 Be considerate of wildlife

Apart from pets, we share space with other creatures, much of it wildlife. People often view these as 'pests' because they encroach on human communities. Millions of animals are killed every year because they are considered a nuisance. In cities, insects, mice, rats, raccoons, squirrels, pigeons (and even feral cats and dogs) are routinely trapped and poisoned. In suburban and rural areas, wolves, coyotes, bears, rabbits, seals, geese and cormorants are also killed in mass numbers for infringing on human activities. Some wildlife is killed just for being an 'eyesore' or ruining well-manicured lawns.

However, almost all the animals we consider 'pests' are either natural to their ecosystems or were introduced to the area by humans. However annoying some animals may be, they have no choice but to inhabit the areas that they do. They may not be beautiful or majestic but they are capable of pain and fear, and often play an important role in their ecosystems.

Encourage friends and family to see the value in all life, and to take positive measures to coexist with wildlife. Simple solutions, like putting away food scraps, securely closing garbage cans, screening windows, and blocking holes in your house, can keep unwanted wildlife out of your space. If an animal does decide to move in (or more likely has become trapped in your home) live-trap it and either release it or take it to an animal sanctuary.

There are many wildlife organizations that are willing to give advice and help with humanely capturing and relocating wildlife.

## 10 Challenge corporate power and support social justice

This book has tried to show the connections between various justice issues. Our global economic system is responsible for the simultaneous exploitation of many groups, including animals, people and environment. These different forms of exploitation do not exist in isolation, but all stem from the same root – a corporate ethic that devalues life. In order to secure rights for animals, we need to challenge economic exploitation in all its manifestations. In addition, protecting humans and ecosystems also directly benefits animals.

For example, when ecosystems are poisoned or destroyed, animals inevitably suffer and die. Likewise, when people don't have access to food, shelter, health care or decent wages, they are less able to defend the interests of animals. Protecting oppressed humans and the environment from exploitation are very important goals in their own right, but they are also essential to the struggle against the human mistreatment of animals.

# Contacts and resources

### INTERNATIONAL
**People for the Ethical Treatment of Animals**
The world's leading animal rights campaign group with offices in the US, UK, Netherlands, Germany, France, and India.
www.peta.org

See also companion websites such as: www.goveg.com, www.caringconsumer.com, www.animalactivist.com, www.petakids.com, and www.petatv.com

**Friends of Animals**
Works to free animals from cruelty and institutionalized exploitation around the world.
www.friendsofanimals.org

**The Meatrix**
Award-winning educational animated film about factory farming.
www.themeatrix.com

**World Animal Net**
The largest network of animal protection societies with consultative status at the UN. Working to improve the status and welfare of animals with over 2,500 affiliates in more than 100 countries.
http://worldanimal.net

**Animal Concerns**
A project of the EnviroLink Network providing a clearinghouse for information on the Internet related to animal rights and welfare.
www.animalconcerns.org

**Respect for Animals**
Campaigns against the international fur trade.
www.respectforanimals.org

**The Animals' Voice**
Good online resource for news and links.
www.animalsvoice.com

### AUSTRALIA
**Animal Liberation Victoria**
ALV is an abolitionist organization dedicated to helping all animals with a strong focus on those factory farmed.
www.alv.org.au

For a complete list of Animal Liberation groups which run autonomously in each Australian state see:
www.animal-lib.org.au/docs/contacts.shtml

**Australian Vegetarian Society**
www.veg-soc.org

**Choose Cruelty Free**
Is an independent, non-profit organization which seeks to promote a cruelty-free lifestyle.
www.choosecrueltyfree.org.au

### CANADA
**Animal Alliance of Canada**
Committed to the protection of animals and to the promotion of a harmonious relationship among people, animals and the environment.
www.animalalliance.ca

**Animal Rights Canada**
Online resource for Canadian activists.
www.animalrightscanada.com

**ARK II**
Seeks to promote and protect the rights of all animals and foster their individual liberties through direct action, political action and public awareness campaigns.
http://ark-ii.com

### NEW ZEALAND/AOTEAROA
**Animal Rights Legal Advocacy Network**
www.arlan.org.nz

# Contacts and resources

**National Anti-Vivisection Campaign**
www.stopvivisection.org.nz

**Save Animals From Exploitation (SAFE)**
www.safe.org.nz

## UK
**Animal Aid**
Campaigns peacefully against all animal abuse, and promotes a cruelty-free lifestyle.
www.animalaid.org.uk

**British Union Against Vivisection**
www.buav.org

**Campaign Against the Fur Trade**
www.caft.org.uk

**League Against Cruel Sports**
Founded in 1924, it is the UK's leading animal welfare group campaigning to end cruelty to animals in the name of 'sport'.
www.league.uk.com

**Protecting Animals in Democracy**
Enables citizens to use the political system and elections to tackle animal abuse and exploitation.
www.vote4animals.org.uk

**Uncaged**
Anti-vivisection campaign group.
www.uncaged.co.uk

**The Vegan Society**
www.vegansociety.com

**Vegetarian & Vegan Foundation**
www.vegetarian.org.uk

**Vegetarians International Voice for Animals - Viva!**
www.viva.org.uk

## US
**Association of Veterinarians for Animal Rights**
www.avar.org

**John Hopkins Center for Alternatives to Animal Testing**
http://caat.jhsph.edu/

**The National Anti-Vivisection Society**
www.navs.org

**Physicians Committee for Responsible Medicine**
www.pcrm.org

**Vegan Action**
www.vegan.org

# Index

# Index

# Index